FAMOUS
FASHION
DESIGNERS

VALENTINO

FAMOUS
FASHION
DESIGNERS

COCO CHANEL

MARC JACOBS

CALVIN KLEIN

RALPH LAUREN

STELLA McCARTNEY

ISAAC MIZRAHI

VALENTINO

VERSACE

VALENTINO

Ronald A. Reis

CHELSEA HOUSE
An Infobase Learning Company

To my sister, Candy Reis, a professional researcher, for her invaluable help in gathering material for this book, and even more so for the encouragement she gave me throughout the writing process.

Chelsea House
An imprint of Infobase Learning
132 West 31st Street
New York NY 10001

Library of Congress Cataloging-in-Publication Data

Reis, Ronald A.
  Valentino / by Ronald A. Reis.
    p. cm. — (Famous fashion designers)
  Includes bibliographical references and index.
  ISBN 978-1-60413-983-9 (hardcover)
  1. Valentino, 1932– —Juvenile literature. 2. Fashion designers—Italy—Biography
—Juvenile literature. I. Valentino, 1932–   II. Title. III. Series.
  TT505.V35R45 2011
  746.9'2092—dc22

  [B]   2010034101

Chelsea House books are available at special discounts when purchased in bulk quantities for businesses, associations, institutions, or sales promotions. Please call our Special Sales Department in New York at (212) 967-8800 or (800) 322-8755.

You can find Chelsea House on the World Wide Web at
http://www.chelseahouse.com

Text design and composition by Lina Farinella
Cover design by Alicia Post
Cover printed by Bang Printing, Brainerd, Minn.
Book printed and bound by Bang Printing, Brainerd, Minn.
Date printed: February 2011
Printed in the United States of America

10 9 8 7 6 5 4 3 2 1

This book is printed on acid-free paper.
All links and Web addresses were checked and verified to be correct at the time of publication. Because of the dynamic nature of the Web, some addresses and links may have changed since publication and may no longer be valid.

Contents

1

Gowns, Glamour, and Grandeur

For decades he has been known simply as Valentino. Although his full name is Valentino Clemente Ludovico Garavani, the internationally renowned Italian fashion designer is so well recognized and respected that his surname was dropped long ago. Pierre Bergé, designer Yves Saint Laurent's right-hand man, has said of Valentino, as quoted in *Couture: The Great Designers*, "I don't know any other Italian designers." Walter Veltroni, onetime mayor of Rome, told Michael Specter of the *New Yorker*, "There is the Pope, and there is Valentino. In this city I don't know who else is as famous."

Indeed, Valentino fits right in with A-list fashion icons such as Ralph Lauren, Pierre Cardin, Yves Saint Laurent, Coco Chanel, Calvin Klein, Karl Lagerfeld, Oscar de da Renta, Christian Dior, Giorgio Armani, and Gianni Versace. "All I ever wanted was beauty—to make women beautiful," the couturier (high-fashion designer) once proudly declared, as reported by Suzy Menkes in the *New York Times*. Without question, Valentino has long since succeeded in doing just that.

Throughout his career, Valentino has dressed many of the world's wealthiest women, movie stars, and crowned royalty. These celebrities love to dress up in the uniform that sets Valentino apart; one that exudes a timeless elegance. The list of the Hollywood elite that Valentino has dressed for award nights and international galas reads like a who's who of the silver screen: Elizabeth Taylor, Julia Roberts, Sophia Loren, Joan Collins, Brooke Shields, Audrey Hepburn, Gwyneth Paltrow, and Anne Hathaway, among others.

According to fashion writer Janie Samet, in conversation with Pamela Golbin, author of *Valentino: Themes and Variations*, "Valentino has managed to turn every fashion model into a lady, and every lady into a fashion model. Being his client amounts to becoming the very incarnation of elegance—true elegance. Did these society figures, princesses, and stars give him all that subtlety and love of detail, or did they suddenly acquire their elegance thanks to his designs?"

No doubt about it, the designs helped—tremendously.

Floral designs take center stage for the expert couturier. "I have paid homage to all the flowers that I love so much through my creations of fabrics and dresses," Valentino said, as quoted in Marie-Paule Pellé's *Valentino: Thirty Years of Magic.* "That was my way of thanking all these marvels that have given me so much pleasure." Valentino's flower motifs are encrusted, stylized, shaped, embroidered, and printed on numerous dresses, always with the greatest thought and caliber.

Animal prints are another favorite form of expression for the Italian designer. Stylized prints that look like hides of giraffes, leopards, tigers, and zebras serve to give his garments an exciting, in-motion look. Equally, geometric motifs, inspired particularly

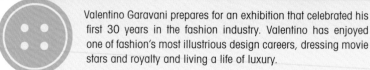

Valentino Garavani prepares for an exhibition that celebrated his first 30 years in the fashion industry. Valentino has enjoyed one of fashion's most illustrious design careers, dressing movie stars and royalty and living a life of luxury.

by Art Deco designs of the 1930s, have served Valentino and his clients well.

Above all, there is that level of high fashion, haute couture (pronounced "ot kutyr") craftsmanship that Valentino's ateliers (fashion studios) are required to adhere to. "With masterful precision, crepes and silk chiffons were pleated, ruffled, and braided to produce silhouettes as light as they were airy, without any loss of the form's essential volume," writes Pamela Golbin. "The craftsmanship Valentino mastered in his youth accounts for his creations of an oeuvre [body of work] successfully designed to pay tribute to the quintessentially active, generous, and self-assured contemporary woman."

For the ever-stunning Valentino woman, wherever formality takes her, she is instantly recognizable. And nowhere does such ritual find greater expression for gowns, glamour, and grandeur, revealed through the couturier's art, than at Hollywood's annual Academy Awards.

Supermodel Reign

They were known as the Celestial Six. Supermodels Naomi Campbell, Cindy Crawford, Claudia Schiffer, Kate Moss, Linda Evangelista, and Christy Turlington shone with supernova brilliance. Every man's desire, every woman's envy, the primadonna "bad girls" of the early 1990s lived lives of unprecedented fame, power, beauty, and, above all, wealth. A disreputable occupation a hundred years earlier, modeling had become a ticket to high society and the only profession in which women earned more than men.

Being young, tall, stunningly beautiful, and, above all, near-cadaver thin wasn't enough to represent a fashion house in the last decade of the twentieth century, however. A supermodel had to have a distinctive "look," an x-factor. Models such as Cindy Crawford were said to have a "love affair" with the camera, of being that All-American dreamgirl. Such luminous beauties signed exclusive contracts with fashion firms, agreeing, in effect, to become their face to the world. A marriage was born—reigning models would form symbiotic relationships with ruling fashion brands; both would, it was anticipated, ascend to the stars together.

The supermodels had been lucky enough to enter the fashion world at a time when alternate "gown hounds," that is, Hollywood actresses, were de-glamorizing themselves. But then the pendulum swung. Consumers tired of seeing the same "Celestial Six" over and over again on the catwalk, on television, and in fashion magazines. And A-list actresses once more became willing to dress up and clamor after a piece of the supermodel advantage. Fashion establishments, particularly those in the exalted business of high fashion (or haute couture, such as the House of Valentino), soon saw gold in Hollywood representation. The days of the supermodel were, if not over, clearly waning—at least for the time being.

MADE FOR EACH OTHER

Although the Oscars and fashion have had a long history together, it wasn't so in the very beginning. At the first Academy Award ceremony, in 1928, Janet Gaynor, the "best actress" winner, wore a store-bought Peter Pan–collared dress. It wasn't long, however, before she sought the advice of designer Gilbert Adrian. The Gaynor-Adrian pairing, it turned out, was just the beginning of a mutually advantageous relationship between actress and designer.

Over the decades, the likes of Givenchy and Audrey Hepburn, Edith Head and Grace Kelly, Halston and Liza Minnelli, Arnold Scaasi and Barbra Streisand, Bob Mackie and Cher, Chanel and Sarah Jessica Parker, and Valentino and Cate Blanchett have gotten together to do each other an obvious favor. Actresses and the show's producers quickly figured out that a fabulous look at the Academy Awards ceremony would lead to tons of glamorous photographs and miles of print. "The telecast has grown into an endorsement worth, according to some estimates, $1 million per gown or accessory in publicity for ateliers (fashion studios), with the potential to make fashion designers into stars in their own right," reported the *Los Angeles Times'* Julie Neigher. Star actresses, star designers—they are a natural fit.

Anna Wintour, the powerful editor of *Vogue*, was one of the first to understand the lure of celebrity actresses married to fashion. In 1997, she realized that stars in designer fashion were a more powerful force in the industry than supermodels such as Naomi Campbell, Cindy Crawford, Claudia Schiffer, or Linda Evangelista. "Magazines began to make A-listers into cover girls, sending their sales skyward," commented Neigher. "By the new millennium, Nicole Kidman had scored a million-dollar deal with Chanel. Clearly the days of wearing your own dress or one provided by the studio wardrobe department were over."

Getting Hollywood's Academy Award nominees and other top industry divas ready for the big night is an arduous task— one given a great deal of thought by stylists and managers alike.

Actress Cate Blanchett wears Valentino on the night she wins the Academy Award for Best Performance by a Supporting Actress in 2005. The designer made the couture gown expressly for Blanchett, who often showcases his creations on the red carpet.

Cristina Erlich, stylist to 2010 lead supporting actress nominee Penelope Cruz, as reported by Melissa Magsaysay of the *Los Angeles Times*, would fly to Europe as early as the previous October to see designer collections before they hit the runway. Couturieres and couturiers (female and male haute couture designers, respectively) were only too eager to welcome her.

All this dressing of the stars in haute couture style is well worth the time, effort, and cost. For many of the viewing and buying public, what is remembered about the Academy Awards is not who won what, but who wore what. For fashion houses, the ensuing publicity is a boon to the sale of their prêt-à-porter (ready-to-wear) and accessory offerings. As Bronwyn Cosgrave suggested in the title of her provocative book on the subject, *Made for Each Other*, this was, and is, a mutually advantageous relationship. No one knows that better than the emperor of haute couture himself—Valentino.

A CUT ABOVE

Not all of Valentino's haute couture clients are stars seeking the limelight. But they are an elite group. "Women wearing Valentino do not toil in factories," Michael Gross wrote in *Valentino's Magic*. "Women wearing Valentino can be found lounging poolside in Capri. Skiing in Gstaad. Running board meetings in Manhattan. They can be anywhere, but they aren't everywhere. Valentino's women make a dinner meaningful and magnificent; they do not make dinner."

Such women, it is apparent, carry themselves with extreme confidence, the assurance that comes with knowing they look as good as it can get wearing a garment that, in many cases, was made strictly for them and will appear on no one else—ever.

"A woman must cause heads to turn when she enters a room," Valentino announced in *Valentino's Magic*. "A woman does not want to disappear. She wants, in the classic interpretation of her power, to make an entrance."

Michael Gross, summarizing the Valentino woman's place in the world, observed that she populates all the best places, knowing that she has what it takes to "pass unmolested through even the worst of times.... Women wearing Valentino are simply a cut above."

Although celebrities are eagerly given haute couture to wear by all the A-list designers, there are those who buy the expensive garments at full price—in some cases for well over $100,000. They don't want the public to know who they are. These individuals, many of whom belong to what is referred to as the "secret society of haute couture," with membership restricted to a select 200 or so, insist on remaining anonymous. Their designers are sworn to secrecy, assured of protecting their client's names and the prices they pay for what is worn. It's all hush hush, exclusive. Such women are used to the best of everything, not just dresses. They seek to be part of the world of glamour.

The women in this elite circle are passionate about fashion. "I felt I was transformed by haute couture," one woman declared in the film the *Secret World of Haute Couture.* "I felt I was transfixed, it puts you in another world, one of refinement, one that is rarefied."

The women of haute couture talk about "wearing a piece of art," of the dress lasting a lifetime, of it never being out of date. The dresses, being so light and airy, make the wearer look years younger. Since haute couture is considered art of the highest level, many women justify the extravagant purchases as a form of investment, as important or unimportant as the best wine, the finest furniture, or the most meticulously crafted object.

When it comes to fashion, no one can give these women of means more of what they want than Valentino. In full recognition of that fact, as far back as 1991, to commemorate the House of Valentino's 30 years in business, the couturier's admirers gathered to celebrate in a manner the likes of which Europe had not seen in decades.

ELEMENTS OF STYLE

*I've always been curious. Art—with a capital A—interests me great-
ly. I can spend hours in museums when I'm on my travels. The museum I like best is perhaps the Rijksmusem in Amsterdam. I have an
unreserved admiration for the great masters: Rembrandt, Velázquez.,
Goya, Bruegel. I'm also deeply moved by the places where paintings
are found, by such imposing objects as the Russian marbles at Len-
ingrad's Hermitage, impressive delftware, the Klimt in the Palais
Stoclet in Brussels, and the sobriety of Hoffmann. I am myself a keen
collector. Sometimes I imbue a dress with the excitement I felt on seeing certain works of art: for example, my collections have included
Russian themes, things by Hoffmann, or Etruscan or Greco-Roman
motifs. Art is an inexhaustible source of wealth and joy.*

—*from* Valentino's Magic *by Marie Paule Pellé and Patrick Mauriès*

THIRTY YEARS OF MAGIC

It was announced in July 1990 that the celebration, "Valentino:
Thirty Years of Magic," would present a monumental exhibition
featuring the couturier's important stylistic periods. It would
be held at the Accademia Valentino, in the renovated Palazzo
Mignanelli, in Rome, early the following year.

Then came the first Gulf War. The international conflict that
erupted in January 1991 was greeted with trepidation everywhere,
including the world of couture. Would the press and dignitaries
that flock to spring-summer fashion shows in the first month of
the year fail to show up? Maybe it was best to cancel such events
altogether?

No! The Paris shows would go on, and Valentino's collection,
his seventh in the fashion capital of the world, was, as usual, exquisite. "In his thirty-year career, Valentino has learned all the tricks of
fashion—cut, detail, craftsmanship . . . for him everything has to be

perfect," wrote Suzy Menkes, of the *International Herald Tribune*. "Valentino's models sprinted down the runway at the Musee des Arts Decoratifs on Wednesday night as if they were race horses," added the *New York Times*'s Bernadine Morris. "They carried their meticulously beaded and appliquéd [decorated] clothes insouciantly [light-heartedly], with the casual ease of sports clothes."

The highlight of Valentino's finale was a floor-length, white, silk dress with the word *peace* embroidered horizontally in silver and gray beads in 14 different languages, including Hebrew and Arabic. A short, white, satin flaring coat with a decorated dove accompanied the dress. The audience went mad with applause.

On June 6, the thirtieth anniversary festivities previously announced (but then postponed because of the Gulf War) got under way. The next day, at the Accademia Valentino, the honored designer cut the ribbon at the show himself. More than 300 styles were on display, brought together not in chronological order, but according to theme. Oscar de la Renta, one of the many fellow couturiers paying homage to one of their own, said that, as reported by Morris, "while the clothes were done over many years [1960 to 1990], they all projected the same strong image: they are always elegant. He obviously has a deep understanding of the women for whom he designs."

The 500 attending party and dinner guests included world-class supermodels such as Dianne DeWitt, Claudia Schiffer, and Linda Evangelista, as well as the likes of Ivana Trump, Marella Agnelli, Nancy Kissinger, and Elizabeth Taylor, who, though arriving late, looked stunning in a shoulder-baring, bouffant Valentino dress.

In September, the "Valentino: Thirty Years of Magic" exhibit crossed the Atlantic to New York City, where it was presented at the Seventh Regiment Armory, which had been transformed into an Italian piazza for the extravaganza. "Placido Domingo's tenor dominated as he, Bette Midler, and Aretha Franklin sang 'Happy Anniversary to You,'" reported Bernadine Morris. "Sophia Loren brought the house down when she swept onstage to receive an award for her work with abused children."

A year shy of his sixtieth birthday, Valentino had clearly obtained all he had ever hoped for—and a great deal more. Fame, wealth, and, above all, achievement were his in abundance. Yet the next two decades would bring still more of all three. Not bad for an Italian kid who had grown up during the international economic depression of the 1930s in a war-torn country run by a fascist dictator.

2

The Apprentice

Valentino Garavani was born on May 11, 1932, in Voghera, a small town south of Milan, in northern Italy. He was named after Rudolph Valentino, the heartthrob silent-screen movie idol of the 1920s. At the time of Valentino's birth, Italy had already spent a decade under the thumb of Benito Mussolini, a fascist dictator. By 1932, the worldwide depression had hit the country hard. And during World War II, Italy sided with Germany and Japan, forming the Axis powers fighting against the Allies: mainly the British, the Americans, and the USSR. In 1945, at war's end, Italy was in defeat and ruin.

Valentino grew up immune to the trials of dictatorship, economic deprivation, and war that most of his countrymen experienced. His mother, Teresa de Biaggi, and his father, Mauro Garavani, seemed to have provided him with the isolation and security that produced an apparently happy, but spoiled, childhood. For the boy, it was a time when an interest in the aesthetic, particularly in fashion, was not only allowed to flourish but also actively encouraged.

At the tender age of 10, Valentino began to demand from his parents made-to-measure clothes, particularly sweaters and shoes. The cashmeres had to have just the right collar and cut. As Patrick Mauriès, writing in *Valentino's Magic*, put it, "At a young age, he [Valentino] chose only to see and to take interest in the 'beautiful and the good.'" Valentino, it seems, already knew what he desired. He later said, as reported by Mauriès, that in his youth he possessed "an almost infantile belief in the possibility of getting out of life what I want."

In the period immediately following World War II, Valentino's sister, Wanda, began to take her younger brother to the movies to see Hollywood films. Valentino was captivated by the likes of Lana Turner, Hedy Lamarr, and Judy Garland, with their jewels and, in particular, their spectacular gowns in the haute couture tradition. Valentino knew where his future lay. Decades later he would declare, as quoted by Valerie Steele in *Glamour*, "I love glamour and I thought 'Oscars.'"

While in middle school, Valentino, with his many freehand variations of fashion design in hand, "apprenticed" under his Aunt Rosa, along with a local designer, Ernestina Salvadeo. In his last year of high school, the designer wannabe told his parents he wished to quit school without taking his final examinations. He wanted to dive right into fashion design. Valentino did complete his exams but insisted that, for him, going to college was not an option. Consequently, with his parents' blessing, Valentino spent a few months in Milan studying French and taking courses in fashion design. Six months later, at the age of 17, the determined and remarkably self-assured youth announced that he wished to go to Paris, the capital of clothing and of, as Mauriès puts it, "hostesses and balls, of the spirit of the time."

FASHION PARADISE

During World War II, clothing was designed and manufactured under wartime restrictions. Skirts were shorter, in part because there was less fabric available. Women were drawn into the workforce (especially at factories) as a replacement for their fighting brothers and husbands. They now predominantly wore pants, all the better to handle the varied jobs at hand. The military look, out of necessity, became *the* fashion during the war years, from 1939 to 1945.

With the fighting over, however, women for the most part were eager to forsake work outside the home. They were happy that their men were alive and home, and they were willing to vacate their jobs for the men to take up again. With clothing, women were tired of what they had been forced to wear. They were ready for a change. Women, particularly in Europe, wanted to exhibit the feminine touch, to look beautiful and sexy, to experience elegance and luxury once more. France, in particular, was only too willing to give them what they craved.

In Paris, the postwar years would become the golden age of the couturier. Through its accredited body, École de la Chambre Syndicale de la Couture Parisienne (School of the Employers' Federation of Paris Fashion), the French government gave official backing to couturiers and all they strived to accomplish. The trade association became responsible for setting the dates of the twice-a-year couture showings, which drew thousands to the French capital. It also established the rules whereby a fashion enterprise could be known as a couture house. To be accepted into the elite category of couture, a firm had to employ a specific number of workers, while staging quasi-public showings for six weeks after the introduction of each season's collections. And, most notably, the house had to be French—foreigners were not welcome.

No one individual was more influential in reestablishing France's dominance in fashion design and fabrication after the war's

Fashion designer Christian Dior poses with two models who wear his creations. Dior's use of excess fabric and feminine adornment was groundbreaking in the post-World War II era.

crippling effects than Christian Dior. In 1947, with his famous and enormously influential "New Look," Dior set out to evoke a happier time. He is to have stated, as noted by Caroline Rennolds

Milbank in *Couture: The Great Designers,* "Fashion comes from a dream and the dream is an escape from reality." Thus, if a woman's life was hard or dreary, by wearing Dior or imitations, she need not show it. She could clothe her body in feminine garments that were the antithesis of a civilian version of a military uniform.

In direct contrast to the fabric stinginess that the war had demanded, Dior became renowned for his lavish and abundant use of cloth. "No less than 25 or 26 yards [75 or 78 feet] of taffeta were needed to obtain the volume of such suggestive named lines as *Corolle, Cyclone, Tulipe, Oblique, Sinueuse, Verticale,* not to mention the 50 yards [150 ft.] of black plait that edged the neck and hemlines of a 1947 model," wrote Mauriès. "Shameless expenditures, exaggerated shapes, and voluminous materials became all the rage in a society that had just emerged from the privations of the war."

Dior's New Look dominated the fashion world for at least 10 years. It was into this universe, in 1950, that the young, energetic Valentino arrived. Knowing full well he was in the right place at the right time, at the center of the fashion world, Valentino enrolled in a school run by the trade association. In addition to study, the couturier-to-be took up dancing and developed a love of French theater. Both would serve him well in developing his design aesthetic in the years and decades to come.

LEARNING FROM THE BEST

While still a student at École de la Chambre Syndicale de la Couture Parisienne, Valentino made a name for himself by winning a competition for fashion design sponsored by the International Wool Secretariat. Karl Lagerfeld and Yves Saint Laurent would win the award a few years later. It was a great start for the 18-year-old Valentino. There would be many more awards to come.

Also during this formative period, Valentino was invited to the opera in Barcelona. There, he was mesmerized by the fact that all the costumes onstage were red. "I realized," he would recall years later, as quoted by Bernadine Morris in *Universe of Fashion: Valentino*, "that after black and white there was no finer colour." In time, red would become Valentino's signature hue.

In 1952, with diploma in hand, Valentino sought out apprenticeships. His first choice was Jacques Fath, then, failing that, Cristóbal Balenciaga, known by his colleagues as a fashion master. For his interview with Balenciaga, Valentino was asked to draw a garment. "It was such a difficult coat—flat in front, big in the back," he was to have said, according to Pamela Golbin. "Stupidly, I started with the front and I couldn't get the line. I was so upset." Balenciaga did not hire him.

Unphased, the fashion graduate soon found work with Jean Dessès, a couturier who, among other things, had royal clientele. Valentino would spend five years with Dessès, a time of 20-hour workdays as well as a time for learning the rules of royal etiquette.

Between helping with window dressing and greeting clients at Dessès, Valentino continued to sketch. If fact, he was hired out by Dessès to Countess Jacqueline de Ribes to sketch her dress ideas, since the stylist could not draw. "He'd [Valentino] come up to my private salon, I'd show him my muslins, he would patiently sketch them," Ribes would recall years later, as quoted in *A Grand Italian Epic: Valentino Garavani*. "This continued once or twice a week for more than a year. We had such fun mixing our worlds."

In 1957, Valentino left Dessès to join Guy Laroche, where he would spend two additional years apprenticing. According to Valentino, one day he met Laroche (whom he had worked with previously) on the street, where the latter declared, according to Golbin, "What? You're still at Dessès? Come work for me!"

In truth, Valentino left Dessès under a cloud. It seems that the good-looking young man, who had an obsession with tanning, had unduly prolonged a vacation in Saint-Tropez, basking in the sun. He was asked to leave the employ of Dessès.

Italian model Marionlina Della Catto wears a white coat, hat, and boots from one of Valentino's earliest collections.

ELEMENTS OF STYLE

Rome is unique: a city where one should not work, but only walk about, seeing the sights and discovering new things all the time. It's a city that takes my breath away. When in Rome, one should take the opportunity to experience the Ponentino, *at that magical hour between day and night, when gentle relaxation at last takes over. It is a city of lights, of colors. It's the city of love—indeed, it is a love affair that never grows stale. Rome is a delightful mistress who makes us feel that we, too, are eternal.*

—*from* Valentino's Magic *by Marie Paule Pellé and Patrick Mauriès*

No matter, working with Guy Laroche proved another valuable experience for Valentino. "As it was a small house, I dealt with everything, and learnt more and more," the young designer remarked, as quoted in *Valentino: Themes and Variations.* "I handled all sorts of things—drawings, dressing the models for the runway, and getting into taxis to go and pick up dresses."

Finally, in 1959, after a formal education in fashion and seven years of on-the-job training, Valentino, then 27 years old, felt it was time to strike out on his own, to open a salon featuring his exclusive designs. To do that, however, Valentino would, at least temporarily, forsake the world's fashion capital, Paris, and head back to Rome.

LA DOLCE VITA

La dolce vita means "the sweet life." Originally, it was the name of a film by critically acclaimed Italian director Federico Fellini. Set in 1960s Rome, the movie tells the story of Marcello, a playboy journalist torn between the sweet life and the serious life. The term, *la dolce vita*, however, soon came to symbolize the high, glamorous life being lived in Rome at the time, when the stars of the jet set came out in full bloom. Elizabeth Taylor was in Rome with Richard Burton to film *Cleopatra*, and Audrey Hepburn and Rita Hayworth, as well as Italians such as Monica Vitti and Sophia Loren, were prancing and partying in the Eternal City. Rome was the place to see and be seen.

Valentino dived into this world by setting up shop at Via dei Condotti 11, a posh locale close to the piazza di Spagna (Spanish Steps). It was a gutsy move for the fashion designer, one that would require the financial backing of his father and an associate. "Why I ever thought I could go out on my own like that, God only knows," Valentino recalled, as quoted by Michael Specter in *The New Yorker*. "But my parents gave me a little money and I started. I had no idea what I was getting into. Sometimes ignorance is a wonderful thing."

In November 1959, Valentino presented his first collection, Ibis, showing off 120 styles. It was met with considerable critical success. Still, Valentino was not pleased with his accomplishment. "The collection," he told Eugenia Sheppard, of *New York Magazine*, as quoted in *Valentino: Themes and Variations* "was full of ideas, but had no personality ... Gradually, everything I did became softer and more elegant."

That said, Valentino knew he was on to something by the publicity he was generating. "My first year, I did a collection, and people were very interested in me," he told Matt Tyrnauer years later, as quoted in *A Grand Italian Epic*. "A new guy, he comes from Paris, and he opens in Via Condotti, with a beautiful collection and some girls. So the attention was there, but I didn't do the right things. I was very naïve."

CHANCE MEETING

The basic outline of Valentino Garavani and Giancarlo Giammetti's first meeting is well known and has been retold countless times in the last half-century. According to Giammetti, six years Valentino's junior, the chance encounter on July 31, 1960, as reported in *A Grand Italian Epic*, went as follows:

"I was in my second year of university, studying architecture, and I would go often to Via Veneto and have an ice cream. You would sit together and see everybody passing by—from 7 o'clock, cocktail time, to 2 o'clock in the morning. Big cars. Here is Sophia Loren, there is Gina Lollobrigida, Marcello Mastroianni, Fellini with Anita Ekberg, Elizabeth Taylor with Richard Burton.

"I was sitting in this café called Café de Paris one evening and I was alone. It was around 11 o'clock and I was waiting for a nightclub to open. I see these three guys arriving and one was vaguely familiar to me. I said to myself, I have seen this guy—who is this? One of them came over to me and said, 'Could we sit with you, because there is no other table?' It was really packed, and the people would fight for a table. I said, 'Of course.' I discovered that one of them was this guy called Valentino, and I remembered that maybe I'd read something about him. Valentino was already a celebrity, as a very, very young designer from

Giancarlo Giametti (*left*) and Valentino (*right*) pose with model-actress Marisa Berenson in 1978. Giametti and Valentino have been partners since they met by chance in 1960.

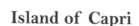

Island of Capri

The four-square-mile (ten-square-kilometer) island of Capri, less than 10 miles (16 km) off the southern coast of Italy in the province of Naples, has been a destination for tourists since the time of the Roman Republic. More recently, Capri has become a haven for artists, as well as a relatively safe place for gay men and lesbians to lead a more open life. For Valentino and his partner Giancarlo Giammetti, the island, famous for sun, blue waters, and a carefree lifestyle, was and still is a place to escape, even if only for a day, when the pressures of work overwhelm.

One of Capri's main attractions is what is known as the Blue Grotto (Grotta Azzurra), which is famous for its size, the incredibly intense blue tones of its interior, and the mystical silvery light that emanates from the objects immersed in its waters. It is easy to see that Capri, with its many attractions and relative isolation from the bustle of Italian peninsula life, would be a playground for the fun-loving, life-absorbing fashion partners Valentino and Giammetti.

Paris. He had opened his first *maison de couture*, and he was in the papers. So we sat and started to talk. And I took him home in my little Fiat."

In the ensuing months, Giammetti regularly visited Valentino on Via Condotti. Soon enough, Giammetti gave up his studies to help his new friend out. Though he had no experience in such matters, Giammetti began to take a keen interest in the business side of fashion, thus freeing Valentino to do the job of designing.

Mauro Garavani's partner, who had invested in the fashion house, was now, after seeing how lavishly Valentino could spend money, having second thoughts. When he demanded his money back, the House of Valentino verged on bankruptcy. Once again, Valentino's parents stepped in, selling their country house to keep the enterprise afloat. The two young Italians, now partners, packed up their belongings and moved to a fresh location at Via Gregoriana 54. They would successfully fight bankruptcy and start a new company. In time, Valentino and Giammetti, having formed a partnership "made in heaven," would conquer the fashion world.

3

Haute Couture

Clothing, it is said, has three basic functions. One wears a garment, first and foremost, for protection against the elements. There is also the issue of modesty, to hide what should not too readily be seen. And, of course, there's the matter of adornment, the need to make an "appearance." Protection, modesty, and adornment, or, as Nancy L. Green declares in her thoughtful book *Ready-To-Wear and Ready-To-Work*, "Clothes are utilitarian, chaste, and pretty. In other words, garments are functional, fashionable, and furnish the figleaf."

In the beginning, and for centuries thereafter, people had to make their own clothing. Fabric had to be gathered, cut, and stitched together. For the most part, this was women's work. "In colonial America, women made their family's clothing after completing their other household chores," writes Sharon Lee Tate, in *Inside Fashion*

Design. "Early American families set aside a room for weaving and sewing. Fashion was beyond the reach of most people. Those who could afford custom-made garments purchased them from dressmakers and tailors who made them to measure, styling them from European fashion plates and dolls. Most fine cloth was imported."

The problem with fashion plates, which were illustrations of fashionable styles of clothing that appeared in magazines in the last half of the nineteenth century, is that they rarely gave any information about the materials or techniques used in the design depicted. It took the dissemination of Ellen Louise Demorest's mass-produced tissue-paper dressmaking patterns, as well as Elias Howe's 1842 invention of the sewing machine, to make productive seamstresses out of ordinary housewives. Curiously, at the very time when the house-bound woman was in a position to efficiently provide clothes for the whole family, ready-made garments were coming into their own. As a consequence, interest in fashion (that is, art applied to clothing) began to spread from the elite to the masses.

Such fashion was quick to convey the rigid differences between the roles of the sexes. As Gini Stephens Frings points out in *Fashion: From Concept to Consumer*, "Men 'wore the pants,' which became a symbol of dominance, while women wore constraining garments characteristic of their restricted life styles and obedience to their husbands and fathers." Frings further notes that with practical, simple clothes for men, most fashion emphasis shifted to women's wear. In turn, women were often criticized for paying too much attention to what they wore. Yet Frings is quick to defend that practice, noting that such interest "seems perfectly understandable, considering that until recently men did not give women the right to own anything else *but* their wardrobes."

For those with the financial means and taste to match, making a dress, or even having it fabricated by the local tailor or seamstress, was not the only option. There existed haute couture, French for "high fashion." Dresses made in the haute couture tradition were exclusive, one-of-a-kind, custom-fitted garments made from high-quality,

This reception or dinner dress in two parts was made by the House of Worth around 1883. Charles Worth is considered the "father of French haute couture."

expensive fabric. They were sewn with extreme attention to detail and finish, almost always using hand-executed techniques. Couturieres, women who created such works of art, had existed for centuries, attending to royalty in most cases. With the arrival of Charles Fredric Worth (1825–1895), however, haute couture became available to a whole new (albeit upper-class) clientele. Indeed, the term *couturier*, the male version of couturieres, was inaugurated to describe him.

THE FATHER OF HAUTE COUTURE

Charles Worth, though an Englishman, is considered the "father of French haute couture." Born in 1826, he began working in a draper's shop at the age of 12. A year later, Worth started a seven-year apprenticeship, selling shawls and dress material. In 1845, at the age of 20, the couturier-to-be left for Paris. In 1858, he opened his own salon. Worth, completely at home in the capital of fashion, would quickly proceed to revolutionize the industry.

Worth's first innovation was to redesign the crinoline, a skirt with extraordinary width, mounted on a cage frame made of steel hoops. It was said that with the crinoline, it was impossible to dress alone; many hands were needed to fit the dress onto a female form.

Worth simplified the crinoline by flattening the skirt in the front, as well as gathering the fullness of the material in the back. The result was a bustle, with its exaggerated "rear end." Though ridiculed by many, the dress became a sensation.

Worth, the first couturier, was convinced that the female body should, as Charlotte Steeling says in *Fashion: the Century of the Designer*, "be both laced up and padded, in order to approach the ideal of the hourglass—delicately fragile at the waist, spreading out voluptuously above and below. In profile, the line followed the shape of the S, more or less sharply curved, according to the corset and bustle."

Worth was the first designer to attain star status by simply signing his garments as though they were works of art. In effect, he developed a "label," the first in fashion history. In so doing, the couturier soon created demand for garments made by him, and him alone. In time, Worth acquired so many clients that he could choose to sell only to the ones who were deemed attractive and prestigious enough to display his clothes to their best advantage. Worth's customers, affluent and with refined tastes, relished being "created" by the master couturier. With some society women needing as many as 40 gowns for a single social "season," Worth became both a busy and wealthy man, indeed. He is still held in high regard today.

The Corset

The nineteenth-century corset, used to achieve a fashionably small waist and at the same time raise the bust, was perhaps the most controversial garment ever created for a woman. Worn under a dress but often over a thin cotton or muslin shift, a corset was usually constructed of whalebone pieces inserted as paneling into a fabric shape. It was then laced tightly at the front or back of the waist. When formed into an S-bend silhouette, the corset reached down over the hips and thrust the bust forward. The corset may have made for an elegant form, but it was severely criticized for endangering the wearer's health and even life.

"The corset-curse among women is more insidious than the drink-curse among men," declared Helen Ecob, author of the popular advice book *The Well-Dressed Woman: A Study in the Practical Application to Dress of the Laws of Health, Art and Morals.* "A woman can no more be trusted with a corset than a drunkard with a glass of whiskey."

Dr. Robert L. Dickinson, the inventor of the "manometer," was the chief proponent of what evil the corset could inflict on a woman's body. The meter he invented, using a scale and a glass tube filled with mercury, was to have shown that the weight of even the loosest corset approximated that of a 25-pound sack of flour. According to the doctor, such constant pressure on the vital organs was harmful, making for rapid heartbeat, shallow breathing, irritability, constipation, and cowardice.

Despite such protests, the corset reached its heyday in the nineteenth century. Yet, as the twentieth century dawned, change was afoot. The boned corset was replaced by woven elastic material that flattened the waist rather than drawing it in. Undergarments in the 1920s heralded the approach of the girdle of the 1930s. And in the 1940s and 1950s, the waspie (an abbreviated corset) emerged to create the tiny waists of Dior's New Look. The corset was all but dead, to the relief of many women.

In another major fashion innovation, Worth introduced the concept of the "collection," where a new round of dresses was presented every year. Thus began the constant factor of change (with its resulting boost in sales) to the fashion industry. It was Worth's ability to create clothes readily attributed to him; to establish the supremacy of his own taste; to basically tell refined women what they should wear, rather than allowing them to decide for themselves, that revolutionized the fashion industry for all time and made his title "father of haute couture" fully justified.

IN HIS FOOTSTEPS

Other couturiers followed Charles Worth, most notably Jacques Doucet and, somewhat later, Paul Poiret.

Doucet, born in 1853, would become one of the best-known and respected couturiers of the late nineteenth and early twentieth centuries. His early playmates were Gaston and Jean-Philippe, sons of Charles Worth. Doucet was predestined, it would seem, to become a fashion designer.

For Doucet, extravagance knew no bounds. He specialized in styling women for grandly staged appearances. Such clients wished to draw the attention of well-to-do gentleman. "Doucet dressed us like good, respectable mothers or like colonels' wives," wrote Liane de Pougy, a famous demimondaines (a woman supported by a wealthy man), as quoted in *Fashion: the Century of the Designer*. Such women were expected to appear fragile, delicate, and, above all, ornamental.

According to Milbank, "Doucet provided such clientele with concoctions made, not surprisingly, of lace and trimmed with other costly confections: silk ribbons and flowers, feathers, braid, beadwork, and embroidery. He used rare gros point de Venise for entire dresses, or re-embroidered panels of more fragile Alencon with pale flowering vines to match the barely tinted silk underneath."

In Doucet's time, it was the stage, more than magazines or a "day at the races," that became a showcase for a couturier's talents. For Doucet, a dress had to be grand and regal. By the time of his death in 1929, such fashion aesthetics were clearly on the decline, however.

Paul Poiret, born in 1879, would wind up working for Doucet and for the House of Worth. He is to have famously declared, as quoted by Steeling, "Fashion needs a tyrant." Poiret, of course, envisioned himself as the fashion dictator, and by the turn of the twentieth century, his influence was enormous. The self-assured, even arrogant couturier would become the first true fashion celebrity.

Poiret saw himself, above all else, as an artist. As Milbank was to remark of him, "He believed that an artist was someone who put himself into everything he did, and he breathed his passion for fantasy and his rare individuality into each endeavor—writing, painting, theatrical and interior design, and schemes for fabrics, objects, scents, and dresses." The couturier could not have agreed with Milbank more. "It was in my inspiration of artists, in my dressing of theatrical pieces, in my assimilating and response to new ideas, that I served the public of my day."

Poiret died in 1944, a year before World War II ended in Europe. Thus, he was not present to see the many changes in haute couture that the war would foster in the coming decades. The mantle of high fashion would, however, be eagerly picked up by the likes of Coco Chanel, Christian Dior, Yves Saint Laurent, Pierre Cardin, and, of course, Valentino. It would not be easy, producing haute couture in a postwar atmosphere where the art, having regained its allure, would require enormous effort and a remarkable attention to detail in its competition with prêt-à-porter.

100,000 STITCHES

Movies, literature, paintings, sculpture, trips—any of these, and more, can be an inspiration for a couturier. Just talking to someone new can also motivate a designer. And such revelation can come at any moment. Creativity and inspiration are unique and personal.

Materials and fabrics are extremely important too. In the 1960s, the development of Lycra inspired designers to create bodystockings and figure-hugging pants. Two decades later, the idea of skintight leggings and cycle shorts resulted from fibers such as polyurethane.

In the beginning, a couturier will usually draw or sketch his designs. For a single collection, a thousand such quick illustrations are often created. It is a time, often the only time, when a designer works alone.

The design figures are then picked up by the *première d'atelier*, a woman who acts as the designer's right hand and who is, next to him, the most important person in his studio. "She is," according to Elke Reinhold, author of *From First Design to Finished Article*, "responsible for communicating ideas and assigning tasks to her colleagues through every single step of the design process. The *première d'atelier* also has to draw design models, bringing the garment to life with the help of the original sketches; she cuts cotton cloth for the first sample; tries it on the dummy, pins it, prepares the basic pattern, and makes the prototype. She is also responsible for the final selection of fabrics, buttons, and other details."

Seamstresses work in Valentino's workroom at the Maison Valentino in Rome. Every couture gown Valentino produces is a result of hundreds of hours of work by several seamstresses.

ELEMENTS OF STYLE

I like women who wear polka dots: they're always fun and even when they're resting, they seem to be moving. Polka dots are for me a basic tool of my trade like all the other classics: gray flannel, plain jersey, tweeds. A fabric with polka dots can be combined with anything: with floral, check, or striped materials. Yes, I set great store by women who wear polka dots. They denote a sense of lightness, of playfulness, of humor, a certain nonchalance, a taste for racy gaiety. Or simply wit.

—*from* Valentino's Magic *by Marie Paule Pellé and Patrick Mauriès*

From the toile, which is the first finished garment in stiff cotton cloth, a prototype is made in the desired fabric. It is fitted on a model again and again until it is as good as it can be. While this stage is being completed, button-makers, pleaters, embroiderers, lace-makers, tulle-makers, and *passementières* (responsible for braiding and trimming) are busy at their tasks.

All of this, creating an haute couture dress, takes an enormous amount of time, and thus money. Hundreds of hours are often put into each dress. In 1988, Yves Saint Laurent, in creating his Les Iris dress, found his seamstresses spending 600 hours at the task. Karl Lagerfeld's Atys creation for Chanel in 1997 required 1,280 hours of work. A single garment can require up to 100,000 stitches, all sewn by hand. A given collection may demand up to 25,000 hours of toil.

In the "golden age" of haute couture (in the two decades after World War II) upwards of 15,000 women were wearing dresses produced in the above manner. Some, such as the Duchess of Windsor and Gloria Guinness, would order whole collections at a time. Immediately before the war, 35,000 people worked in haute couture houses. It was into this world of elite fashion creation that Valentino was now privileged to enter.

FLORENCE TRIUMPH

For Valentino, la dolce vita, the sweet life of affluence and decadence infusing Rome in the early 1960s, when the international darlings of the film industry happily congregated, represented an opportunity. It was a time when Hollywood stars discovered the couturier. Valentino wanted to be the designer they gravitated to.

"Valentino and I met in Rome in 1960 during the shooting of *Cleopatra* and I became one of his first clients," recounts Elizabeth Taylor, in *Valentino: 30 Years of Magic.* "He designed my clothes for *Ash Wednesday* and *Night Watch.* I've been wearing his clothes in my private and personal life ever since. I got hooked—his clothes are addictional."

Elizabeth Taylor dances with Valentino at his anniversary party celebrating 30 years in the fashion industry. A highly visible movie star, the glamorous Taylor brought attention to Valentino's designs in the 1960s.

It was Valentino's subsequent association with celebrities, such as Elizabeth Taylor, that would give him the exposure and fame he needed to reach his true destiny as a couturier. Valentino knew that with the likes of Elizabeth Taylor frequenting his salon, his extravagant designs would become a form of theater that, as Patrick Mauriès noted, "is never better interpreted than by the incredible, exaggerated, filtered, altered humanity that is conferred by celebrity."

Still, for the young Valentino and Giammetti just starting out, breaking into the fashion establishment would not be easy, celebrity contacts or not. After all, the two were still novices, breaking new ground as they went along.

As luck or guile would have it, though, in 1962, two years after meeting Elizabeth Taylor, Valentino would score in a way that Hollywood would be hard-pressed to fabricate.

"When we started, our first shows were in Rome," Giammetti relates in *A Grand Italian Epic*. "Then I discovered that the most important show would be in Florence. . . . We go to see this famous man called Marchese Giorgini, who was the big patron and boss of the Florence show. The Florence show was very important—all the American buyers would go and that's where the Italian designers Simonetta and Fabiani would show things to be copied for America.

"So Mr. Giorgini said, 'I heard about this nice guy, Valentino.'
'Yes, yes.'
'You want to come show?'
'Yes, yes.'
'I can give you this time.'

"I look at the calendar—it was the last day and the last hour. I said, 'Can I have something better?'

"He said, 'No. Take it or leave it.' So we took it."

The rest, as is so often said, is history.

The American buyers, for the first time, stayed to see Valentino and bought many of his clothes. As the couturier recounted in *A Grand Italian Epic*, "From that moment, of course, I showed in Florence every year, and they gave me better hours, a better place."

As momentous an event as the Florence show was for the new partners, later in the year an equally fortuitous happening occurred. Valentino had made up an ensemble for Gloria Schiff, the twin sister of Consuelo Crespi. The latter worked in Italy for American *Vogue*. One evening, Consuelo called Valentino from Rome and told him that Gloria had worn one of his dresses to a party where Jacqueline Kennedy was in attendance. The First Lady was crazy about the outfit Gloria was wearing. She wanted to know who designed it.

For a couturier on the rise and out to garner all the attention he could get, it wouldn't, it couldn't, get any better than that.

4

The White-on-White Collection

By 1963, Valentino and Giammetti had become known as the *due ragazzi,* or "two boys." They began to travel to the United States on a regular basis, several times a year, to show their designs. A traveling fashion show really hadn't been done before. The partners met with important buyers from leading department stores, as well those who represented upscale boutiques. They reached out to the media. And the two took every opportunity to make the acquaintance of elite society figures, such as Jayne Wrightsman, Gloria Guinness, Babe Paley, and the Duchess of Windsor. Some of these soon-to-be clients made a habit of changing clothes—expensive, haute couture garments—three or four times a day. From Los Angeles to Palm Beach, to Chicago, to New York, the *due ragazzi* were an aggressive pair, indeed. They were out to make their mark—and they would.

Giammetti told Pamela Golbin, as reported in *Valentino: Themes and Variations*, that Valentino came to America almost seasonally because he was paid to design collections there. "He earned a great deal of money that way. I remember the day a buyer from Bloomingdale's called me to order fifty little red coats.... We also had major buyers, people like Miss Martha who, with her three boutiques in New York, Palm Beach, and Palm Harbor, had an extremely wealthy clientele. We sold 300–400 dresses per season to her alone! Money began to pour in, and soon made the Valentino firm's fortune. Our labor costs were so reasonable that we were able to turn out couture clothes at the price of ready-to-wear."

Valentino's 1963 fall-winter collection displayed features reminiscent of Renaissance gowns, those with high waists, padded shoulders, and sleeves fitted seven inches (17.7 cm) below them, reported Dino Buzzati in *Valentino's Magic*. "I rather like it, but most of the professionals shook their heads, as if the innovation were too dramatic.... One cannot travel in the subway like that; rather, it was as if all the subways had disappeared from the face of the earth and immense Cadillacs respectfully awaited the ladies in their Valentinos, solemn as Infantas [princesses] of Spain."

It was at this time that the seedbed of Valentino's fashion style began to emerge. It would grow into what Suzy Menkes, fashion editor of the *International Herald Tribune*, defined as "Franco-Italian." "If you define the essence of Valentino's work, it is also the definition of Rococo: exquisite flourishes developed from a sculpted base," Menkes commented in *A Grand Italian Epic*. "It is evident in the designer's tailoring, when a jacket has a lacy collar or a skirt breaks out into ruffles at the hem. The dresses are pure Rococo with their millefeuille [puffy] layers and decorative details."

Gloria Schiff, senior fashion editor at *Vogue* from 1963 to 1971, was quick to sum up Valentino's contribution to fashion when she said of the times, as quoted in *A Grand Italian Epic*, "You know, everyone in Paris was doing very constructed clothes, like Balenciaga, Givenchy. Everything was shaped and modeled, and tight

Valentino sits in his studio before releasing his fall collection. With a growing list of international celebrity clients, the young designer was quickly becoming famous in his own right.

and constricted. Valentino was the first to do clothes that really enhanced a woman and moved with her—made her look sexy, provocative, and alluring."

Valentino, it had become obvious to an ever wider, more influential audience, really cared about couture.

THE JACQUELINE KENNEDY CONNECTION

Jacqueline Kennedy was just 30 years old when her 42-year-old husband, Jack, was elected president of the United States in November 1960. The young couple brought instant style and glamour to the White House. For the inauguration on January 20, 1961,

Jacqueline had American designer Oleg Cassini create a wardrobe that, she told him up front, should make her look like she was the wife of the president of France.

In terms of style, Jacqueline Kennedy's designers sought to bring her personality to the fore by, among other things, never overshadowing her face with veils or hats. The rules of etiquette often demanded that a woman wear a hat in public. Mrs. Kennedy found a designer to invent one just for her. The small hat, called a pillbox, was worn perched on the back of her head. When the First Lady accidentally dented her hat one day, similar hats with dents suddenly became "the thing."

The ultimate Jacqueline Kennedy outfit, one to flatter her boyish figure, became the unadorned shift dress. The First Lady's style forswore patterns in favor of solid, usually pale colors. What she wore became the essence of simplicity and reserve.

All the glamour surrounding Jacqueline Kennedy came to a tragic end on November 23, 1963, when John F. Kennedy was assassinated in Dallas. The picture of the First Lady, in her blood-splattered Chanel suit standing next to Lyndon B. Johnson as he was being hastily sworn in as president, will never be forgotten by those who were alive at the time. Refusing to take the dress off, Mrs. Kennedy remarked, "The whole world should see what they have done to Jack."

In September the following year, Gloria Schiff found herself playing tennis with Kennedy, who was still in full mourning for her slain husband. Kennedy turned to Gloria and was to have said, as quoted in *A Grand Italian Epic*, "Honestly, even if I wanted to go out, I have nothing to wear." Gloria responded, "Look, I don't want to push anyone on you.... But Valentino's in town, and I know he'd love to show you some of his clothes. If you want, I can call him for you."

Valentino jumped at the opportunity to meet Jacqueline Kennedy; he went to her apartment along with a model. The former first lady was a perfect size for high fashion: She stood 5 feet 7 inches (170 centimeters) tall, had a long waist and small chest, and weighed between 120 and 130 pounds (54.4 and 58.9 kilograms).

Valentino quickly gained the trust of former first lady Jacqueline Kennedy, just after the assassination of her husband. Here, the two sightsee in Italy.

She fit right into the model's clothes. She ordered six garments, all black and white.

According to Schiff, the purchases Kennedy made lifted her spirits so much so that she started going out again. Being photographed by paparazzi everywhere she went, wearing Valentino, boosted the young designer's reputation. In addition to the publicity she provided, Jacqueline Kennedy would become Valentino's muse for years to come.

Fashion Photography

Fashion photography is a field all its own, a genre of photography dedicated to displaying the items of fashion: clothes and accessories. It is heavily devoted to advertisements in magazines such as *Vanity Fair, Allure,* and, of course, *Vogue.*

Fashion photography, as so defined, first appeared in the early twentieth century in such French magazines as *La mode practique.* In the United States, *Vogue* and *Harper's Bazaar* competed to produce the most eye-catching and alluring images of the gowns they advertised. It was at this time that house photographers, many of them European, such as George Hoyningen-Huene, Horst P. Horst, Edward Steichen, and Cecil Beaton, transformed fashion photography into a true art form.

In the post–World War II period, it was photographer Richard Avedon that revolutionized fashion photography and thus redefined the role of the fashion photographer with his imaginative images of the modern woman. Of his work, Harold Brodkey has said, as quoted in *Avedon: Photographs 1947–1977,* "His photographs are always photographs, and they do not play sentimentally with the stillness of the photographic image—the unearned or mechanical stillness. In Avedon's photographs, that stillness is ravaged by motion, the hint of motion, or feeling: that is to say, emotion."

Throughout the 1960s, Avedon worked for *Harper's Bazaar.* During the 1970s and 1980s, he switched to *Vogue* and, in the process, took some of the most famous portraits of those decades. In 1994, a retrospective of his work, "Richard Avedon: Evidence," was presented at the Whitney Museum in New York City. Avedon was voted one of the 10 greatest photographers in the world by *Popular Photography* magazine and in 1989 received an honorary doctorate from the Royal College of Art in London. He was to have famously said, as quoted in *Avedon: Photographs 1947–1977,* "All photographs are accurate. None of them is the truth."

A YEAR FOR WHITE

The 1960s would turn out to be quite a decade for Valentino, with 1968 in particular a year like no other—for Valentino and for the rest of the world.

With calls for peace, love, and hippie utopia building as the decade progressed, 1968 was reality check time. It was a year of deep tragedy, pain, and anger around the world. January saw the Tet Offensive in Vietnam, resulting in a realization for America that the Vietnam War was, indeed, going to be long and costly. In May, university students and teachers in Paris walked out of classes in general protest, yelling, "Be reasonable, demand the impossible." A national strike ensued that nearly toppled the Charles de Gaulle government. And in Czechoslovakia, the reformist administration of Alexander Dubček was brutally crushed by Soviet tanks, ending the short-lived "Prague Spring." In the United States, civil rights leader Martin Luther King Jr. was assassinated, as was presidential candidate Robert F. Kennedy, brother of slain president John F. Kennedy.

Throughout it all—the drama, the upheaval, the misfortune—Valentino's career moved ever forward. In the first month of the year, the couturier unveiled in Rome his spring-summer ensemble, which became known as his white-on white-collection. Garments consisted of coats, dresses, striped sweaters, chiffon, organza, lace-embroidered stockings, and scarves draped around the neck. All were almost completely white. With the January show, Valentino instantly became the "king of fashion."

"At that time, in 1968, the collections were not small, like today," the designer commented decades later, as quoted in *A Grand Italian Epic*. "People were delighted to be in the audience, and they enjoyed seeing endless collections; they would not get bored staying seated for an hour-and-a-half, seeing dresses constantly going up and down. So the collection was very big. And when you see 150 exists [models wearing gowns on a runway], it's a lot; and most of them all white. It was a shock because nobody had ever done something like this."

Vogue called Valentino's white collection "the talk of Europe" and commented on "The cleanliness and distinction of his crisp whites, his lacy whites, his soft cream whites, all shown together white-on-white." Gloria Emerson, writing in the July 16 issue of the *New York Times*, sang out, "Valentino's white does not mean the chalk color that needs a good tan, or the famous Courrèges sheet-white that looked so antiseptic. His white is the color of Devon cream, and the palest girls will be able to wear it."

An ardent admirer and herself a fashion arbiter of considerable influence, Eleanor Lambert went so far as to declare the white collection "dazzling," according to Matt Tyrnauer, while adding, "It proved [Valentino] has the stature of changing the world of fashion mood overnight." Electrifying words, indeed, in praise of a man not yet 36 years old—and not even French.

THE WEDDING DRESS

Soon after her husband's death, Jacqueline Kennedy began to fear not only for her own life but for those of her children, Caroline and John. There were threats and the constant presence of the paparazzi wanting to capture the famous widow's every move. In response, Kennedy sought out what privacy she could for herself and her children.

In June of 1968, when her brother-in-law Robert F. Kennedy was assassinated in Los Angeles after winning the California Primary for president, Jacqueline remarked, according to Seelye Katherine of the *New York Times*, "If they are killing Kennedys, then my children are targets.... I want to get out of this country."

Although during her widowhood Kennedy was romantically linked with a few men, notably Roswell Gilpatric and David Ormsby-Gore, nothing came of these relationships. Then she met Aristotle Onassis, probably the wealthiest Greek shipping magnate of the twentieth century. Twenty-five years her senior, the two nonetheless fell in love—or so they wanted the world to believe. In truth, the marriage that followed was one mainly of convenience. In exchange for a considerable sum of money,

Jacqueline Kennedy boosted Valentino's publicity by wearing one of the designer's creations for her wedding to Greek shipping magnate Aristotle Onassis.

ELEMENTS OF STYLE

For me, white is *a color! White is one of the things that brings me luck. I remember the 1967 collection that I dedicated to Jackie Kennedy, for whom I designed 12 white dresses. It was a formidable success. I always like white because it stands for the lightness of summer, for purity. White can be used in such different ways. I can remember an old box of white lace that had been given to one of my aunts by Countess Asti; it was the purest joy. It was the box of lace that gave me the idea of painting the stockings of models with lace patterns— back in the sixties. At the time there were only plain stockings, so I started a new trend. White also stands for dreams.*

—*from* Valentino's Magic *by Marie Paule Pellé and Patrick Mauriès*

Kennedy agreed to the arrangement. In addition, she got something even more valuable—the privacy and security she so desperately wanted for her family.

On October 20, 1968, on the Onassis private island, Skorpios, in the Ionian Sea, Jacqueline and Aristotle were married. From the marriage, Valentino would receive perhaps the greatest gift of all, at least as it pertained to his career. On the momentous day, Jacqueline wore a Valentino wedding dress.

Since, at the time, she was buying virtually all of her clothes from Valentino, the media, in its frenzied speculation, assumed Jacqueline Kennedy would wear a Valentino creation for her wedding. They were right. Kennedy chose her dress from the "white collection" the couturier had assembled earlier in the year.

"She chose a particularly simple design, consisting of a high-necked, long-sleeved blouse with horizontal lace appliqués and a short pleated skirt of ecru crepe georgette; the subtle contrast between the style's two pieces made it a most distinctive choice," wrote Pamela Golbin. "It was a sensation."

Immediately after the wedding, the House of Valentino received orders for no less than 60 copies of the dress, all high fashion, all couture.

As a result of the unprecedented publicity now engulfing Valentino, the couturier was thrust onto the international stage.

EXPANDING HIS INFLUENCE

The year previous to designing Jacqueline Kennedy Onassis's wedding dress, Valentino received the prestigious Neiman Marcus Prize in Dallas, Texas. Four days later, he accepted the Martha award. Valentino was no longer seen as a Roman couturier. He was now entering the worldwide fashion consciousness as a superstar designer of the first rank.

In 1968, Valentino launched his "V" label, with the letter appearing as a decorative element in his dresses. Gloria Emerson of the *New York Times*, says, in *Valentino's Magic*, "Valentino has climbed to the peak of success during the last year, because of the colors and the materials he uses, but above all because he is a volcano of new ideas, which, good or bad, are entirely his own."

By the early 1970s, it was no longer enough for Valentino to be a name in fashion. Along with Giammetti, the partners were now ready to take the next logical step—to create a Valentino *brand*.

5

The Valentino Brand

As the House of Valentino grew and prospered in the 1960s and 1970s, interested parties sought out Valentino or Giammetti with offers to purchase, or at least to secure an interest in, the fashion enterprise. "In 1967, a shoe company called Beck—a very large company—approached us asking if we wanted to sell," Giammetti recalls, as quoted in *Vanity Fair*. "We decided on a certain price, which I don't remember exactly, but it was around $5 million. So we go there, ready to get this *huge* amount of money. For us it was huge. And the guys from Beck didn't show up. Instead a lawyer came, saying, 'Unfortunately, we are not going to go through with it. We didn't get the money.'"

The Beck deal wouldn't be the last acquisition effort to go sour. In 1969, the House of Valentino was actually sold. Robert Kenmore, an entrepreneur, was behind what was to be a luxury conglomerate. He proposed to buy Cartier, Mark Cross, Georg Jensen, Kenneth Jay Lane, and Valentino, among fashion houses. His wanted to open a shopping center, with all the luxury brands in one convenient location. Giammetti agreed to the deal.

The arrangement did not last long, however. In 1971, the conglomerate filed for bankruptcy. Yet, Valentino and Giammetti were able to buy back their fashion house on extremely favorable terms. Indeed, they had sold the company for $5 million and were able to retrieve it for a "mere" $1.5 million. Giammetti again assumed the role of CEO.

As impressive as the House of Valentino was becoming, at the time the partners were still on a steep learning curve, still improvising, still doing for themselves what a much larger firm would have hired others to take care of. Advertising is a case in point.

"Valentino had designed a collection and he wanted a desert setting," recalls Gian Paolo Barbieri, a well-respected fashion photographer, as quoted in *A Grand Italian Epic*. "We looked for some sand in Rome and I remember that they brought the sand from the Tiber [River]. But it was completely white; it was impossible to work with. So I decided to buy bags of semolina, which is a yellow flour. I made a construction in an apartment below Valentino's office in Rome, and I made dunes out of the semolina. They were made of food, but looked more real than sand."

Valentino and Giammetti did it all. They didn't have an agency to handle the advertising or do the photography, and they didn't have a director to put together the shows. By the early 1970s, Rome, in a regressive stage, was witnessing the end of la dolce vita. The city was becoming more provincial and less international. The partners understood this, and they knew it was time to move on. With boutiques in Milan and New York, Valentino and Giammetti had made a start in reaching out. But in order for the House of Valentino to truly blossom, it was clear it would have to return to the capital of fashion—Paris. In 1975, Valentino opened two

Valentino poses with his partner Giancarlo Giammetti (*right*). Being honest about their romantic partnership wasn't always easy, especially in provincial Italy.

boutiques in the French capital. And for the first time, he showed his ready-to-wear collection in Paris instead of Italy.

THE FRIENDSHIP

The two never told their mothers or fathers that they were gay. Of course, their parents would come to know it in time. In the conservative family environment of provincial Italy in the 1930s, 1940s, and 1950s, the subject of homosexuality was not openly discussed or even acknowledged. "We never talked about it," Giammetti told Matt Tyrnauer in an interview published in *Vanity Fair*.

Giammetti acknowledged to Tyrnauer that when he quit college to join Valentino in his fashion enterprise, it created a scandal in the younger man's hometown. "My father was one of those playboys in Via Veneto—everyday, macho men. But this was more difficult—a guy who goes to work in fashion. Fashion was not seen as a serious business the way it is today, and you didn't want your 19-year-old son suddenly going to work for an unknown designer.... But within a few years they understood not just the passion I put into my work but my relationship with an extraordinary person."

In Italian, *binomio* means "duo." With a company, it means "associates." "In our case it probably is a miracle," says Giammetti, in *A Grand Italian Epic*. "It is synonymous with 'miracle.' Because I've never seen two people so close, and for so many years, without being married. I've seen Valentino almost every day of my life.... An extraordinary association between two human beings."

"I believe in destiny a lot," said Valentino to Tyrnauer. "It was destiny that evening when I was in Via Veneto and met a certain person. Immediately I liked him very much and I told him he had a fantastic character."

VALENTINO'S EXTENDED FAMILY

According to the American Kennel Club, a pug is well described by the phrase *multum in parvo,* which means "much in little," or in this case "a lot of dog in a small space." The animals are considered playful, even-tempered, outgoing, and loving. They are said to exhibit great charm. In Europe, pugs were known for centuries as a "fashionable" breed. No wonder Valentino has owned and loved pugs for decades.

The Devil Wears Prada

In the 2006 film The *Devil Wears Prada*, actress Meryl Steep plays Miranda Priestly, a hard-driving, tyrannical, fashion magazine editor who imposes impossible demands on her subordinates. The highly successfully movie was based on a novel by Lauren Weisberger, who worked for Anna Wintour, longtime editor in chief of *Vogue*. Miranda Priestly's character was supposedly based on Wintour's infamous reputation (she is known by her detractors as "Nuclear Wintour").

Wintour, herself, was the subject of a full-length 2009 documentary, *The September Issue: Anna Wintour & the Making of Vogue*. In the film, director R.J. Cutler follows Wintour and her *Vogue* team as they prepare the five-pound (2.2-kg), 840-page September 2007 issue of the magazine for publication. While Wintour emerges as the demanding editor she is (with zero tolerance for small talk and virtually no willingness to suffer fools) she is also seen as a boss who gets things done, with a great deal of creative genius thrown in.

Naturally, the two films, one fictional, the other real, have been compared. "For the past two years or so, Wintour has been on the media warpath to win back her image," said Paul Schrodt of *Slate Magazine*. Manohla Dargis of the *New York Times*, said, "Priestly had helped humanize Wintour, and the documentary continues this."

Anna Wintour, who dropped out of high school at the age of 15, and then again, from fashion school, when she famously declared, "You either know fashion or you don't," entered the field of fashion journalism in 1970 at *Harper's Bazaar*. By 1986, she was editing British *Vogue*. In 1988, Wintour became the editor in chief of *Vogue* in New York, achieving her lifelong dream job. She has remained a fashion industry power broker ever since.

It is not known when Valentino acquired his first pug, but today he has six. The mother is Molly, and her two sons are Milton and Monty. Three daughters are named Margot, Maude, and Maggie. There have been others in the past, of course. "He's always had pugs," Lynn Wyatt, a longtime friend of the couturier, said, as quoted in the Bennett Marcus blogpost "It's Valentino Day!" "I mean, they die, and he gets more pugs, and he's just always had pugs, and when they snore, he loves it, and when they snort, he loves it."

In 1987, his pug Oliver became the emblem of Valentino's prêt-à-porter line of clothing. He has had no hesitation in dressing a number of his pugs in couture garments of his own design.

When traveling, three cars are usually needed to move Valentino's entourage, especially when heading for the airport to board a private, 14-seat jet. One car carries Valentino and Giammetti. Another takes the staff and the luggage. A third car transports five pugs. One pug, Maude, always goes with Valentino himself.

Often, Valentino is embarrassed to be seen traveling with the pugs because they attract so much attention, something the designer gets plenty of as it is. He usually asks assistants to take the pugs out of the car in two shifts so there seem to be fewer animals.

The pugs are family. As such, though, they compete with a host of humans that make up Valentino's extended, expanded clan, both in his professional world and his private one.

"In fashion houses there's a constant turnover, but they keep people forever," commented Isabel Rattazzi in *A Grand Italian Epic*. "But if people leave, they take it personally. . . . They have so much passion for everything they do."

"Valentino and Giancarlo see their enterprise as much as a family as a business," observed Bob Colacello, as told to Matt Tyrnauer. "Their employees are protégés to be groomed and promoted, then kept as friends even when they venture out on their own."

Actress Gwyneth Paltrow summed up well the relationship between the partners, their friends, and the business when she said to Matt Tyrnauer, "They're sort of another world, especially

Valentino.... But he has such a big heart—he really does—and he's very sensitive. And Giancarlo's just true-blue loyal. That's not to say that he won't, like, hock me to do Valentino's store openings and whatnot. They are Italian businessmen. But they're amazing."

MORE THAN A NAME

By the mid-1970s, the House of Valentino had concluded that in order to make real money, it would need to expand into fashion-related commodities. The first accessory was a perfume named *Valentino*. Of course, the launch of *Valentino* was not an ordinary affair. It was introduced at the Théatre des Champs-Elysées in Paris in October of 1978. After the show, a gala dinner for 260 guests was held at Maxim's and a gigantic buffet at Le Palace, a favorite Parisian nightclub.

From perfume, it was on to full-blown licensing and franchising. There would be luggage, handbags, umbrellas, handkerchiefs, ties, belts, and shoes, just to name the obvious products to carry a Valentino logo. In Japan, where the number of license deals would exceed 35, there were even pens, furnishings, and cigarette lighters. In all, at the licensing peak, there may have been 70 or more agreements.

According to Robert Bruno, Valentino's former assistant and longtime licensing designer, as quoted in *A Grand Italian Epic*, "All the designs came from Valentino. From his collection we would take some details—like roses, or bows: we would take his bow and try to transfer it on bags, shoes, umbrellas.... But he [Valentino] wanted to see everything.... So everything that was on sale had been seen by Valentino."

Although the licenses brought in a ton of revenue, at a certain point it was feared that they would cheapen the brand and it would suffer.

"It was fun, though," Giammetti told the *New York Times* decades later. "Oh I need two million more dollars this year, what can we do? Let's do bathrooms." And they did, with Valentino

ELEMENTS OF STYLE

When I dream of preparing my collection, my immediate thought is of an evening dress; if the concept of work comes into the picture, then I think of a day-time outfit. That's because it's much easier to imagine a woman walking across a ballroom than an active type who has to get through the whole working day and emerge triumphant. The daytime part of a collection calls for a lot of technical research; it's a very important part because it represents the hallmark, the essential character of a fashion parade. The 'Belle de Jour' has to be even more remarkable because hers is an environment of less artifice. The daytime beauty needs to display her self-confidence unflaggingly for a great many hours on end. That's why I feel it's up to me to give her a carefree image.

—*from* Valentino's Magic *by Marie Paule Pellé and Patrick Mauriès*

entering everyone's private sanctuary. "We did loose covers in a fabric—something like a coat from Prada, very fluffy—that were used to cover the toilet," Giammetti continued. "We did that. I didn't even consider how ridiculous it was. For me, it was fun."

It was enjoyable for Valentino too. "I was happy to do the home furnishings and bed linen and other things—every detail," the couturier told Matt Tyrnauer of *Vanity Fair*. "Because I love houses and automatically I was thinking about this for other people. But, finally, after I did children's clothes and baby clothes—no, no, it was too much."

Still, it was with licensing that Valentino and Giammetti got rich. Even though, when the House of Valentino was sold for a second time in the late 1990s, and had, by then, pared their licensed products down to three—perfumes, sunglasses, and jeans—the purchasing price was approximately $300 million. From both a design and business perspective, the partners were doing well indeed.

CLOTHES WOMEN WANT TO WEAR

Sensuality, delicacy, glamour, and *grandeur* are four words often used to summarize Valentino's approach to dress design, a course he has practiced and displayed his entire career. "When I start putting together a collection, my ideas automatically progress along parallel lines," Valentino told Pamela Golbin in February 2008. "That is, I first think of a sublime and wonderful hieratic type of woman who will show my dresses on the runway; but right after that I think of all the women in the world

Valentino poses with models wearing his spring-summer 1997 prêt-à-porter collection. Throughout his long career, the designer's overriding style has been feminine and glamorous. His creations make women look their best.

who can wear them. Yes, I do want my dresses to be worn by real women, whether they are beautiful or not so beautiful, but attractive; for what I look at with great attention is not so much physical beauty. Some women have a great deal of character and incredible charm merely due to their intelligence, the way they speak and move or react. And that is worth all the elegance in the world."

By all accounts, Valentino's approach to design, his methods and attitude, had, by the late 1980s, resulted in an extraordinary body of work. As actress Anjelica Huston told Brad Goldfarb, of *Interview* magazine, "Wearing Valentino is like getting a haircut. His clothes might look like a whisper but they're so carefully thought out and constructed that they can hide a myriad of ills. What he does is magic."

Valentino has noted that a number of his fellow designers will often become contorted with stress during their designing process. Not Valentino. "I'm not tortured, I'm sorry," he told Stephen Schiff, of *The New Yorker*, in 1994. "I want to be happy when I design a dress. And I'm very happy when I create something that I like— something very, very beautiful."

This calmness, assurance, and confidence in just who he is has led others to consider Valentino rather conventional. Valentino, it seems, remembers the 1960s and 1970s quite clearly. "I never took any drugs in my life," he told Matt Tyrnauer, as quoted in *A Grand Italian Epic.* "Not even a taste, smoke, anything. And at many, many parties I would find myself alone in a huge living room, seated on a sofa, because everybody used to disappear. I've always been, and still call myself, a very square person."

6

Ready-to-Wear

By the mid-1970s, if not sooner, Valentino and Giammetti had come to recognize that their fashion world was undergoing a fundamental change. Haute couture, a method of designing and fabricating a dress of unequal quality, was splendid, desirable, and, above all, produced a beautiful, exquisite garment. But a haute couture dress, by its very nature, is for an exclusive client, one with money and influence. Valentino and Giammetti knew that if a fashion house in the haute couture tradition were to survive and grow, it would have to proceed beyond high fashion. The enterprise would need to produce clothes that were more affordable, and thus more accessible, to a wider clientele. Valentino, it became clear, would have to design, create, and, if necessary, license ready-to-wear, or prêt-à-porter, clothing. The 1980s trend away from the tailor and the dressmaker toward the mass producer had nonetheless been in evidence for more than a century.

E. L. Brentlinger, an early fashion critic, was to have said a hundred years ago, as quoted in *A Perfect Fit*, "One-third of your life is spent in bed, two-thirds of your life in clothes." By the latter part of the nineteenth century, Americans first, then Europeans, wanted to wear more clothes, with greater variation. They did not want, however, to spend their precious out-of-bed time making them. Men and women, urban and rural, were increasingly willing to buy clothes already made for them.

Women, in particular, were eager to shun hand-me-down clothes for those designed and fabricated to their liking. Such individuals were quick to sing out with Fanny Brice, in her poignant signature song,

> It's no wonder that I feel abused,
> I never have a thing that ain't been used.
> I'm wearing second hand hats, second hand clothes,
> That's why they call me Second Hand Rose.

Thanks to the growing ready-to-wear industry, donning an older sister's dress would soon become unnecessary. Used-clothing stores, as a result, witnessed a steep decline.

To be sure, made-to-order did not disappear overnight. Indeed, both made-to-order and ready-to-wear continued to exist in tandem, and do so to this day. Still, the growing availability of ready-to-wear in retail stores, particularly the new department stores, was, by the late nineteenth century, altering American dress.

A further accelerator of the ready-to-wear trend occurred with the emergence of catalog houses. As Milbank observed in her book *New York Fashion*, "Clients sent in their measurements, according to the directions given, and could order anything from walking suits to dinner and bridal dresses, mourning clothes, underwear, hats, shoes, shawls, and wraps, as well as dress materials, laces, and trimmings. Ready-made clothes, which could be ordered simply by bust size and skirt length, as opposed to the dozen or so measurements required for made-to-order, cost about the same as the cheapest custom clothes."

By the early twentieth century, both sexes, but women in particular, had taken to purchasing what they wanted to wear. Sewing was becoming a hobby, not a necessity. The ready-to-wear revolution, however, did not suffer from lack of criticism. With all these clothes and styles, with the latter often changing yearly (if not seasonally), many wondered if women were becoming "slaves to fashion."

MARY'S LITTLE SKIRT

"A president can be deposed, an autocrat can be assassinated but against the tyrant fashion neither votes nor bombs are weapons," thundered *Independent* magazine in pre–World War I America, as quoted in *A Perfect Fit*. Fashion "slavery" was clearly on the defensive, with some at the time calling for, as Joselit put it, "a new Temperance Union that would strive to overcome not only King Alcohol but Dame Fashion."

Others objected to the loss of art that they saw in fashion's "decline" to ready-to-wear. Emily Post, the nation's authority on all things tasteful, was to have turned her nose up at the thought of wearing a mass-produced garment. Ready-to-wear was seen as freakish, and certainly not a work of art. Critics, furthermore, insisted that ready-to-wear bred uniformity at the expense of individuality, that the garments so produced ignored the contours of the human body in favor of doll-like dimensions. Wearing them threatened to lower the nation's self-respect.

Then there were the supposed health issues. It was said that mass-produced clothes harbored "disease-breeding" germs nestled in the tucks of a shirtwaist or in the hem of a skirt. The garments were made, critics insisted, in unclean and unsafe shops, which, no doubt, was often the case.

More sinister than microbes, however, was the threat ready-to-wear posed on the moral health of American women, it was claimed. "Disaster seems to strike when women seek to dress as stylishly as those they see about them in the shops or on the streets," Joselit quotes a cynic at the time. "Ready-to-wear," its detractors insisted, "took advantage of the female consumer, especially her perennial concern over being in—or out of—style, and made her a slave to fashion."

Finally, the issue of immodesty rose up. Mrs. John B. Henderson, a prominent Washington, D.C., hostess, surveying the flapper dress of her time, in the 1920s, noted, as quoted in *A Perfect Fit*, "The skirt that trails in the dirt gathering germs is a menace to its wearer's health; but the skirt that flaps around the knees is pretty much of a menace to the modesty of the women who wear it."

Women shop for off-the-rack clothing at a mass-market store in the 1930s. Ready-to-wear clothing changed the fashion industry tremendously.

Vogue

It has been called the most influential fashion magazine in the world. Referring to the book, *In Vogue: The Illustrated History of the World's Most Famous Fashion Magazine*, book critic Caroline Weber, writing in the *New York Times*, declared:

> *Vogue* is to our era what the idea of God was, in Voltaire's famous parlance, to his: if it didn't exist, we would have to invent it. Revered for its editorial excellence and its visual panache, the magazine has long functioned as a bible for anyone worshiping at the altar of luxury, celebrity, and style. And while we perhaps take for granted the extent to which this trinity dominates consumer culture today, *Vogue*'s role in catalyzing its rise to pre-eminence cannot be underestimated.

Vogue began publication as a weekly in 1892. In 1909, Condé Nast took over the magazine and began publishing it every two weeks. Condé Nast sent *Vogue* overseas in the early 1910s, with its most

The indignation addressed at women of immodest attire is perhaps best summed up by a humorous little ditty, "Mary's Little Skirt," composed by Dr. John Roach Straton, a pastor:

Mary had a little skirt,
The latest style, no doubt,
But every time she got inside
She was more than halfway out.

Ready-to-wear, or prêt-à-porter, proceeded at a different pace in France than it did in the United States. Some statistics are successful effort being in the home of high fashion, France. Today, *Vogue* is published monthly in 19 countries.

In 1988, Anna Wintour became editor in chief of American *Vogue*. On the inaugural cover under Wintour's editorship, a three-quarter-length photograph of Israeli supermodel Michaela Bercu, wearing a bejeweled Christian Lacroix jacket and a pair of jeans, was presented. Such an image departed from previous covers that insisted on showing only a woman's face. According to *Time* magazine, the new cover gave "greater importance to both her (a woman's) clothing and her body. This image also promoted a new form of chic by combining jeans with haute couture."

While there has been criticism of Anna Wintour's reign as *Vogue* editor, Amanda Fortini, writing in *Slate*, argued that her policies have been beneficial for *Vogue*:

> When Wintour was appointed head of *Vogue*, Grace Mira-bella had been editor-in-chief for 17 years, and the magazine had grown complacent, coasting along in what one journalist derisively called, 'it's beige years.' The magazine had become boring. Among Condé Nast executives, there was worry that the grand dame of fashion publications was losing ground to upstart *Elle*, which in just three years had reached a paid circulation of 851,000 to *Vogue's* stagnant 1.2 million. . . . . Wintour radically revamped the magazine

revealing. By 1890, 60 percent of garment production in America was in ready-to-wear. By 1951, 90 percent of Americans were buying their clothes "off-the-rack." In contrast, at the same time in France only two-thirds of what was worn by women came from stores. At the twentieth century's midpoint, French women still frequented their small, neighborhood dressmakers to purchase what they needed. The local couturiere persisted.

To a significant extent, the French adherence to couture can be explained by their insistence on the notion of "good taste." Prêt-à-porter was seen as a necessary evil, a come-down for what the artistic-loving French were famous for—designing and making quality, one-of-a-kind clothes that would elevate the fashionable female. This rarified attitude would, of economic necessity, soon have to be modified and, in some cases, discarded altogether.

HAUTE COUTURE MEETS READY-TO-WEAR

Many post–World War II French designers, though wedded to haute couture, were more than willing to embrace the world of prêt-à-porter. Building on the cachet of their high fashion tradition, couturiers such as Christian Dior and Jacques Fath began creating clothes for new, ready-to-wear collections as early as the late 1940s. Some of their garments were actually made in New York, an acknowledgment of the excellence of American workmanship.

As prêt-à-porter took hold, various lines developed and came to be presented on a city-wide basis in twice-yearly fashion weeks. Collections for autumn-winter were shown early in the year, usually in February. Spring-summer collections were exhibited around September. Today, such ready-to-wear collections are offered earlier and separate from haute couture lines.

By the early 1970s, the leading Italian fashion houses that were based in Florence began to show their newly created ready-to-wear lines in Milan, where labor costs were lower and garments could be more quickly and cheaply produced. Paris still held the lead in haute couture, but as ready-to-wear and even mass market clothes took hold, it was not the only place where fashion was occurring.

Valentino and Giammetti, to their credit, were not content to rest on their laurels. In 1974, Giammetti chose the French firm of Mendès, the only manufacturer in France specializing in haute couture ready-to-wear, to fabricate their first prêt-à-porter garments. Mendès was already working with Yves Saint Laurent, Guy Laroche, and Jean Dessès.

The agreement signed between Valentino and Mendès, on December 11, 1974, resulted from tough negotiations. With his deal with a French firm, Valentino was now in a position to do what no

Valentino offered this peach evening gown as part of his spring-summer collection in Rome in 1974. The designer's gowns are always stunning, always feminine, and virtually timeless.

other non-French design firm had up until then been able to do—show a prêt-à-porter collection in Paris. No Italian designer, in particular, had ever been able to prosper in Paris on a lasting basis. As Bernardine Morris, writing in the *New York Times*, observed, "The French are notoriously inhospitable to fashion intruders."

On April 9, 1975, Valentino showed his fall-winter collection at L'Hôtel George-V in Paris. The show generated a sensation, as well as a controversy. "Valentino created waves of admiration at his first show in Paris," commented Alison Lerrick of the Associated Press, as reported in *Valentino's Magic*. "Milan is indisputably No. 1 as the capital of Italian prêt-à-porter. What is in dispute, however, is that the No. 1 Italian designer shunned Milan for Paris to show his new Boutique collection."

THE 1980s LOOK

The 1980s were a good decade for Valentino. In 1985, he celebrated 25 years in the business, in grand style, of course. But while femininity was definitely back, haute couture was increasingly on the

ELEMENTS OF STYLE

Just as I can get enthusiastic about one of those big butterflies that I like so much, I can completely fall for a woman who's dressed quite simply, but has the audacity to draw attention to herself with some small detail, this becoming so remarkable that the way she's dressed no longer matters. Some out-of-this world detail invented by a woman will make her more important to me than one dressed up in all the colors of the rainbow, who just looks ordinary. For instance, a woman wearing a sweater who has the nerve to pin on it a handkerchief covered with sequins or colored stones can make my day. I like women who realize that something quite small can become everything.

—*from* Valentino's Magic *by Marie Paule Pellé and Patrick Mauriès*

defensive. There were many, both in and out of the fashion industry, who thought its days were numbered. Valentino, in some ways, was among them. "My seamstresses have been here for a long, long time," the designer told Matt Tyrnauer. "They are the last dinosaurs, making this type of haute couture.... They are extremely meticulous and they are really old fashioned. It's very rare to find people who work like this."

Indeed, haute couture seamstresses, by the mid-1980s, were clearly an endangered species. There were no younger ones coming up, willing to do the painstaking work in putting upwards of a hundred thousand stitches in a garment. "Why would a woman want to sit eight hours a day with an eye loupe sewing and embroidering a pattern?" Valentino asked Michael Specter, of *The New Yorker*.

VALENTINO RED

When it comes to Valentino's attraction to the color red, there is some slight confusion as to its origin. There is little doubt, however, that the defining event took place in Barcelona at the opera, when the future master couturier was 17 years old. In one account, Valentino explains, as quoted in *Valentino's Magic*:

"I remember one of the most striking impressions I ever had in my life: it was in Barcelona, when I was a student. I'd been invited by a friend of mine to the opera where with fascination I beheld, in a box, a very beautiful grey-haired woman dressed in red velvet from head to toe. Amid all the colors worn by the women she appeared to me to be unique, standing out in all her splendor. I have never forgotten her. For me she became the red goddess. Something fabulous. I think a woman dressed in red is always magnificent. In the middle of a crowd, she is the quintessence of the heroine."

In a second version of the opera story, Valentino told Bonizza Giordani Aragno, as quoted in *Valentino's Magic*, "I started to fall in love with this color [red] during my first visit to Barcelona when

A model presents a design from Valentino's fall-winter 2003 ready-to-wear collection in Paris in 2002. Red has become Valentino's signature color.

I was seventeen years old. A friend took me to the opera; it was the start of the season. The women perched in the boxes around me seemed to be a garland of red flowers. They all wore something in red, and it struck me. That image came back to me when I started to design."

Either way, a woman (or women) in red made a lasting impression on Valentino at a very early time in his career. In 1981, Brooke Shields wore a red organdy evening gown to highlight Valentino's spring-summer collection. By the end of the decade, the color had come to define him.

Red is a primary color. It is a stimulating color. Red is synonymous with warmth and energy. It exudes strength and passion. Red is always contagious, rousing. And, Little Red Riding Hood wore red, thus placing her between innocent and seductive. Of course, there is violence too—red, after all, is the color of blood.

Valentino's trademark red, known as Rosso Valentino, is today a combination of 100 percent magenta, 100 percent yellow, and 10 percent black.

For Valentino, red and flowers have always formed a dynamite combination. "I shouldn't like to go through life without flowers," the couturier is to have said, as reported by Patrick Mauriès, in *Valentino's Magic*. "I love being surrounded by them; so often, they are a sign of joy.... Flowers, for me, are a great source of inspiration; I like to reproduce them on a dress, turning a woman into a bouquet.... I have paid homage to all these flowers that overwhelm me with their beauty in my creations of fabrics and dresses." It is no surprise that poppies, red poppies, are Valentino's favorite flower.

7

Valentino's
Luxury Lifestyle

"**N**obody lives like Valentino," Doris Brynner (a former model) told Matt Tyrnauer. "I don't know anybody who lives as grandly as Valentino." Brynner was referring, in particular, to the many mansions Valentino owns, in Europe and America. But she could just as well have added the 152-foot (46.3-m) T.M. Blue One yacht the designer has, the 14-passenger private jet at his disposal, or the art treasures that any first-rate museum would drool to acquire. "He enjoys every second of it, every square inch and every mile," Brynner continued. "He enjoys everything he has. . . . Valentino loves beauty; he loves everything that's beautiful. He loves everything he has, which I can't blame him for. I mean, the opulence is unbelievable."

John Fairchild, publisher of *Women's Wear Daily* from 1960 to 1996, said, as quoted in *A Great Italian Epic*, "For two people

[Valentino and Giammetti] in the fashion business, living well is the best revenge. Every other designer looks and says, 'How do they live this way?' Yachts, houses, paintings, entertaining, castles—none of the other designers are living that way. . . . There were times when he didn't have any money, but he always lived well and he loved living well."

Valentino and Giammetti have never felt the need to justify their extravagance, not only because they insist they have earned their money, and the right to do with it what they want, but also because they see doing so as an occupational necessity of sorts. The reasoning is based on the observation that as the partner's business expanded, couture itself was contracting. Thus the very world of couture had to be reinvented, and it was left for Valentino and Giammetti to do it. They were required to show (by example, of course), rich, carefree, and young people how to live. "I think what's also extremely seductive is that Valentino lives the life," commented Hamish Bowles, European editor-at-large for *Vogue*, as quoted in *A Grand Italian Epic*. "His clothes look the way they do because he understands how his clients live—because he lives like that, and, in most instances, better than they do."

Living the sweet life doesn't hurt the House of Valentino's image. One thing works with the other. "You know, if they are on a boat, and certain people are on the boat, they get photographed, and that works [to their advantage]," Isabel Rattazzi, a prominent New York socialite, is to have explained to Matt Tyrnauer. "When they're in Gstaad it's the same thing. Most of their friends are big celebrities, anyway, so of course they're going to be photographed. But I don't think it is intentional—they truly like people. It's not like: 'Oh, I'm going to invite that person, so the picture gets taken, and I can sell three more dresses.' I don't think it works that way at all."

Giammetti admits that the two have had fun creating a glamorous image and lifestyle. It was all natural, he insists; nothing was part of a strategy. To hear Giammetti tell it, they were just two kids playing and having fun, while being a bit more ambitious than others.

Valentino stands by a desk in his atelier in Rome, surrounded by beautiful things. His success has allowed him an opulent lifestyle that some consider over the top.

OVER THE TOP

Valentino's mansions, in Rome, in Gstaad (a village in Switzerland), in Capri (an Italian island), in New York, and in London, are nearly as famous as the designer himself. Of them, Pamela Golbin declared, "His charm and sensibility help re-create the atmospheres of classic Hollywood sets. Every single one of his homes is a reflection of the dream he has made come true."

The villa in Rome is tucked into arbors that lined the route Julius Caesar took when entering the city. The Chalet Gifferhorn in Gstaad is a ski lodge where the designer and close friends often spend Christmas. The apartment in New York is near the Frick museum, overlooking Central Park. And in London, Valentino owns one of the largest private houses in the exclusive Holland Park area. Michael Kelly supervises these vast estates, each of which has a staff of 30 to 40. He goes from house to house, arriving a few days before his boss makes his entrance. As has been said, "Nobody lives like Valentino."

Yet, of all the places Valentino has acquired, none approaches the Château de Wideville, an eight-bedroom, seventeenth-century palace near Versailles that originally belonged to a minister of King Louis XIII. Valentino acquired the "dwelling," with its 300 acres, in 1995. He would later receive a prestigious award from the French government for restoring the property to its full glory.

Château de Wideville is surrounded by a moat and flanked by two low houses. It contains some of the most lavish gardens in Europe, with acres of lilacs, lilies, freesia, sunflowers, irises, impatiens, daffodils, wisteria, and gardenias. There is what many agree to be the largest rose garden in the world—with acres of roses in nearly every color. "I don't want to exaggerate," Valentino told Michael Specter of *The New Yorker*, "but do you know how many roses there are here? A million. Not tens or even hundreds of thousands. But a million."

Wideville has its own parish church. The estate is what most people envision when they seek to conjure the opulence of seventeenth-century France.

In describing Wideville, superlatives know no limit. "For me, that house in Wideville is one of the most perfect houses I've ever seen," said designer Tom Ford, as quoted in *A Grand Italian Epic.* "It's perfect because somehow it's not stiff and it's not pretentious.... The scale of the rooms is not ridiculous, and it is lived-in

Valentino's Big Family

Valentino has always valued family. He moves surrounded by a court of friends which has become a real family for him. The group always consists of Giancarlo Giammetti; American bag and jewel designer Bruce Hoeksema; Brazilian brothers Sean and Anthony Souza, as well as their parents Carlos Souza and socialite Charlene Shorto de Ganay, Souza's ex-wife, who are both Valentino's public relations (PR) people. Giammetti confided to *Vanity Fair* that, "this family has stayed together because of me, because when Valentino gets mad he cuts—that is that. I remember when Carlos left and moved to Brazil and married Charlene. Valentino refused to speak to him, but I always talked to Carlos. Then one day Carlos called and said he had a baby boy, Sean. I handed the phone to Valentino, and he started to cry and cry."

Throughout his career, Valentino has, of course, been inspired by many glamorous women. Some of them have become close friends, making up what is referred to as the Valentino's "family." This includes Spanish socialites Nati Abascal, a former model who was married to the Duke of Feria, and Rosario of Bulgaria, the wife of Prince Kyril of Bulgaria. According to *YourNewFragrance.com,* "Valentino met Nati Abascal in 1968 at a party when she was a 19-year-old model and brought her to Capri. Rosario of Bulgaria met Valentino in her native Majorca in the 1990s via Carlos Souza at a club." Another close friend of Valentino is his former PR manager French-Brazilian Georgiana Brandolini, who worked for Valentino for 18 years before leaving for Balmain and ultimately starting his own fashion career.

and livable. And he uses it, he loves it, he enjoys it. And you can sit on anything, you can smoke in the house and he doesn't make you take your shoes off when you walk in. It's incredible to me—his perseverance with perfection and the constant chasing after perfection in everything that he touches."

When asked what it cost to restore the castle and gardens over a five-year period, Valentino whispered to J.J. Martin, of *Harper's Bazaar*, "Let's not speak about it." Upwards of $5 million is often mentioned.

Of all Valentino's incredible properties, it is not difficult to see why Wideville is his favorite.

HAVING FUN

Valentino and Giammetti are more than capable of having fun, enjoying themselves wherever they are. That said, the island of Capri, famous for love and romance, not to mention its pure Mediterranean lifestyle, was, perhaps, the place where Valentino, early in his career, began to truly taste the good life.

"Living in Capri," Valentino relates in discussion with Matt Tyrnauer, "I remember working all week with my collections and having to take a train at 6:30 on Saturday morning to be in Naples at eight o'clock. I had this boat, a Chris Craft, called *San Marco*, and it was waiting for me at the Port of Naples to take me to Capri.... We used to go on the sea all day long, coming from Rome at six o'clock in the morning, having lots of fun, lots of nice girls and boys on board, and picnics on the sea. At seven o'clock in the evening, we would go back to Capri, to stay in the piazzetta for a drink. Then we'd go home for more fun and amusement."

At this time, the late 1960s, Valentino, as would be his style, took to embellishing the 50-foot (15.2-m) Chris Craft he owned. "I decorated it," the couturier recalls. "It was red and white, with lots of pillows. I remember I did all the pillows—very Pop, with lips, cigarettes, hearts, everything." Valentino would go on to own a succession of boats, each one bigger and more elaborate than the

Valentino's entourage includes Giammetti (with the designer, *above*) and many other friends he considers "family." The designer has luxury homes around the world.

previous one. Today, his home on the water is the *T.M. Blue One*, named for his parents, Teresa and Mauro. From stem to stern, it is 152 feet (46.3 m) in length.

The *T.M. Blue One* is outfitted with brass and mahogany and has plush wool carpeting, white sofas, and blue pillows, each one embroidered with the boat's insignia. The boat (some might say ship) contains five staterooms and two espresso machines. It has an art collection ranging from Picasso to Andy Warhol. The *T.M. Blue One* requires a full-time staff of 11 to keep it afloat and cruising about.

According to Michael Specter, writing in the September 26, 2005, issue of *The New Yorker*, beginning late in May, Valentino rents a jet every weekend and flies to wherever the *T.M. Blue One* is docked. In the summer, the boat works its way around the Mediterranean, proceeding wherever whim dictates, to places such as Saint-Tropez, Cap d'Antibes, Ponza, and Portofino, as well as Greece or Turkey. Then, in August, when the fashion business shuts down, Valentino will spend an entire month at sea. The couturier does so, he explained to Specter, because he has no alternative. "I am a prisoner. My staff in Rome, in London, in Paris, even in New York—they are all gone. I cannot go anywhere. I am stranded."

Nobody, it really need not be said again, lives like Valentino.

THE ENTERTAINER

Valentino has said, "There are really only three things I know how to do well: design a dress, decorate a home, and entertain guests." When it comes to the last of the three, when putting on a party or a dinner, it is universally acknowledged that the couturier has no equal.

Valentino gained his appreciation for the better things in life, particularly food, from what, he is quick to admit, was a spoiled, pampered upbringing. "Unfortunately, I am a very difficult person to take around," Valentino told Cathy Horyn, of the *New York Times*. "When I go to restaurants, I'm always upset because the food is not what I like. I don't eat. I just touch two beans."

At home, in Wideville, it is a different story. "In my house, I want everything simple and made with good, organic ingredients," Valentino told Horyn. "We use butter only where you need to use butter, in cakes. My chef is really a creator. If I say to him, 'Frederique, this week, really, I don't want desserts,' he'll make a chocolate cake without eggs or sugar. This is what I love—simple food but very well prepared. Sometimes simple things are the hardest to do, like a little black dress."

Simplicity, along with pure opulence, was on full display the night Valentino hosted 150 people at Wideville for a dinner like no other. Michael Kelly, in charge of the gala event, selected 32 dishes: several types of pasta, four fish dishes, lamb, two northern Italian casseroles (one with shrimp, and the other with chicken). For dessert, there were four cakes, homemade ice cream, several types of chocolate, and profiteroles. To provide a grand entrance, the estate driveway was lined with 1,500 votive candles, placed a meter or two apart.

As the guests began to arrive, it was discovered that one important person had, unaccountably, been left off the list. Both Valentino and Giammetti saw this as a major crisis. Another person of lesser importance was removed from the head table, and the forlorn guest slotted in. According to Specter, "A calligrapher—on duty for just this sort of mishap—was called to correct the error. By the time the unfortunate man's Mercedes rolled up to the gate, Kelly was there to greet him."

Commenting on what it takes to create such an event, with incredible food, entertainment, and guest accommodations, Kelly told Specter, "These days, a private house is run like a Relais &

ELEMENTS OF STYLE

Traveling always stimulates desires; or rather, the desire to travel moves me to depict the images that various countries may produce. The inspiration that the world offers me is unlimited, but over the years the way of expressing it has completely changed. I hate the period around 1970, because all fashion designers, including myself, were too close, too faithful to the themes that inspired us. Nowadays, I know that I react like a painter. I am freer, more detached, vis-à-vis such influences. Nevertheless, all manner of things may attract me: Hungary, Bavaria in Ludwig's day, China, or some kitschy show I happened to see in a faraway land. But the result will not so closely resemble the thing that inspired it.

—*from* Valentino's Magic *by Marie Paule Pellé and Patrick Mauriès*

Chateaux hotel. We have plans, and budgets, and computers to keep track of it all. There is no more landed gentry. These days, even the wealthy work. So they are at their country houses maybe on weekends or once in a while or rarely. But when they are here they expect everything to be the way they want it. This is all very personal for him [Valentino]."

MORE IMPORTANT THINGS

It is easy to dismiss all the opulence and grandeur of what is the quintessential lifestyle of a rich and famous man. At one level, it can seem so frivolous, so unimportant, so fake and phony. But neither Valentino nor Giammetti have ever been accused of being artificial or counterfeit. They are rich and indulgent but also very "real."

Actress Gwyneth Paltrow is quick to relate an incident that, in her eyes, clearly shows the humanity and thoughtfulness of both Valentino and his partner. "They're very generous people and not only with their money and their house," she told Matt Tyrnauer. "I had my 30th birthday at Giancarlo's house. . . . And then two days later, my father started to get really sick. They helped me in ways that—I mean, he was dying, and they sent a helicopter and they hooked him up with the right doctors. And I stayed at Giancarlo's house and they sat up with me—you know, chain-smoking and drinking coffee, waiting for the doctors to call. Really, when the stuff hits the fan, you could not wish for better friends than them."

In 1990, Valentino, together with Giammetti and Elizabeth Taylor, founded L.I.F.E, an association for the support of AIDS-related issues. The initials stand for *Lottare, Informare, Formare, Educare*—to Fight, to Inform, to Form, to Educate. Much of the money raised to attack the disease is gathered through the activities of the Accademia Valentino, a cultural space located near Valentino's atelier in Rome. The Accademia would eventually come to house, among other artifacts, Valentino's archival collections.

Valentino disembarks his yacht in 2001. He has long used his yacht to entertain celebrities and royalty, understanding that it is beneficial to his image and his business to have important people photographed on his boat.

As Valentino approached his sixtieth birthday, life was good. Fashion, and all it produced for Valentino, had led to a life few could even imagine. And yet, in a revealing comment made to Matt Tyrnauer, Valentino tried to keep it all in perspective, to show a humble side that is always beneath the surface. "I am so interested in so many things that it's a pity not to have the time to do them. But it's not just frivolous things. I would also love to take care of some charities. You know, there are some things that are more important in life than a ball with a big gown, or haute couture, or a dinner for 150 people."

8

The Last Emperor

ashion, for many on the outside looking in, is often perceived as frivolous, girly, and passive. Critics know, of course, that there is a whole world of fashion, that a major industry is founded on it, and that a huge range of occupations encompass it. But fashion is, to the cynics, anyway, commonly seen as mystifying, peculiar, and, while glamorous, in many ways elusive. Guy Trebay, writing in the introduction to *Runway*, captured fashion's incredible diversity, and eccentricity, when he asked:

"Is it an atelier populated by madcap designers and their harried assistants? Is it a magazine office filled with super thin editorial adepts? Is it a modeling agency where chain-smoking agents sit at pod-like desks while pimping their human products? Or is it a Hong Kong sweatshop, a factor's front room, a cutter's table, a mediator's office in Chapter 11 proceedings, the vapor of the zeitgeist, the whirl of chi-chi cocktails, the particular clinic where the beautiful strung-out 16-year-olds are sent for a quickie rehab?"

As Trebay goes on to inform us, it is all of these eclectic forces— and more. The many, varied facets of fashion converge, sometimes as often as eight times a year, in a hassled, yet vibrant place known as the fashion show.

"It is all over in 40 minutes: intelligence, talent, effort, ambitions, ideas, projects," Natalia Aspesi declares in *Valentino: Four Days in Paris*. "The splendor of the catwalk, the sashaying of the models, the succession of clothes, the silence or buzz of the specialized audience (journalists and buyers), cold, merciless, all-powerful, yet also prone to excitement, determines the success or failure of a designer, the sales turnover of a company, the work of a lot of people."

In other words, for a fashion designer, and Valentino is no exception, the fashion show is the most important moment in a career. It is classic make-or-break time.

The author, the director, or, above all, the dictator who reigns over the fashion show is the "great tailor," the couturier, the decider. Reporting on Valentino's October 1994 final fashion show rehearsal at the Ritz in Paris, the most famous hotel in the world, Aspesi declares, "Valentino who always has the final say, is the only one who is never tired, who never gets cross, who seems to delight in re-admiring his creations."

Backstage for the show itself, "Anxiety, chaos, crowds of people, fragrances and sweat: each model is beset by two quick and careful dressers, a hairdresser, a make-up artist, and privileged photographers and journalists," Aspesi explains. "Valentino, who checks every exist from head to toe, remains calm and unfurled."

Following Valentino's triumphant "Valentino: Thirty Years of Magic" celebration in 1991, the couture continued to produce and prosper throughout the 1990s. In 1993, the Chinese government invited Valentino to present his collection in Beijing. In 1995, the

A model displays a Valentino gown during the presentation of his haute couture collection in Rome in July 2007.

mayor of Florence awarded Valentino a special prize for Art in Fashion. And in 1996, Valentino was granted the rank of Cavaliere del Lavoro—the equivalent of knighthood. By decade's end, opinion polls showed Valentino to be the most famous fashion designer in the world.

BOUGHT AND SOLD

Naturally, the sharks, the buyers, the acquirers began to gather again. The House of Valentino, by the late 1990s known as the Valentino Fashion Group (VFG), was worth not millions, but hundreds of millions of dollars. In 1998, HdP (Holding di Partecipazioni Industriali), a conglomerate based in Milan, bought VFG for a reported $330 million. At the press conference announcing the deal, Valentino (according to Sara Gay Forden, of *Women's Wear Daily*) broke down and cried.

The partners sold 100 percent of the company to HdP, received a huge cash buyout, and retained 1.3 percent of HdP in shares. Valentino and Giammetti would still be designing and managing, respectively.

Valentino agreed to the sale because he knew it was important to the advancement of his company. "We wanted to develop," Giammetti said, as reported in *A Grand Italian Epic*. "And we knew—I knew—that without a big corporation you cannot survive alone today. That's the only reason we sold. We didn't need the money; we didn't need to give up our work. I wanted to have people help me develop in a world where two people could not do it alone."

Giammetti also recognized that the world of fashion as a business was, as the twentieth century closed, undergoing a fundamental change, one that flipped its priorities—business first, fashion second. "The change manifested itself," Giammetti told Cathy Horyn of the *New York Times*, "when fashion became such an important matter that it became an asset for people who are

(continues on page 92)

Valentino Interview

In April of 2009, 14 months after he retired, Valentino agreed to answer a series of questions put to him at VanityFair.com:

What is your idea of perfect happiness?
No telephone calls.

What is your greatest fear?
To get very sick and not have a fast death.

What is the trait you most deplore in yourself?
I am not able to delegate to others what I know I can do faster myself. It's the impatient Taurus in me.

What is the trait you most deplore in others?
The lack of manners.

What is your greatest extravagance?
To have five pugs and travel with them.

What is your current state of mind?
Much more relaxed than when I was designing eight collections per year.

What do you consider the most overrated virtue?
Fidelity.

On what occasion do you lie?
When I am wrong.

Which living person do you most despise?
Too many choices; too many failures in this world.

What is the quality you most like in a man?
Courage.

What is the quality you most like in a woman?
Courage.

Which words or phrases do you most overuse?
"Voilà."

What or who is the greatest love of your life?
My work.

When and where were you happiest?
Among my very close friends.

Which talent would you most like to have?
The art of the accountant.

What do you consider your greatest achievement?
That I was one of the designers who helped make Italian fashion known everywhere.

If you were to die and come back as a person or thing, what do you think it would be?
A butterfly. They are free and don't get old.

What is your most treasured possession?
The portrait of Eleonora di Toledo made by Bronzino.

What do you regard as the lowest depth of misery?
To be sick and poor.

What is your most marked characteristic?
Optimism. And the concept that nothing is impossible.

What do you most value in your friends?
They have to love my designs!

Who is your favorite hero of fiction?
The Wizard of Oz.

Who are your heroes in real life?
My parents.

What is it that you most dislike?
Cruelty to helpless animals.

How would you like to die?
In my sleep.

What is your motto?
Everything is possible: "Yes you can!"

(continued from page 89)
in finance. Before the banks were behind the big men, like Mr. Arnault or Mr. Pinault. Now the banks want to be in front. They want to be involved themselves."

In the decades following the company's first sale in 1969, Valentino and Giammetti prospered, finding numerous and creative ways to make money. "When Kenmore left, we really grew the business in the normal way—by selling clothes," Giammetti explained to Horyn. "In the 80s, licensing completely changed everything. That lasted until the early 90s. You could make a fortune. Just from royalties from Japan, we were making $12 million a year. You didn't want to know what they were doing, okay. But if you had to prostitute yourself in order to make something better in another field, then you chose one country, and, at the time, Japan was the country most open to licensing."

The HdP deal, like the Kenmore agreement before it, did not last. In 2002, the Italian textile firm Marzsotto bought VFG for $210 million. "They [HdP] had a completely old-fashioned sense of fashion," Giammetti told Tyrnauer. "They didn't know anything about fashion. They believed fashion is a little show with models—beautiful girls they would like to know—walking on the runway. That's it. They didn't know how much was behind it or how important for the company the image of the founder and the designer himself is."

In 2007, the Valentino entity was once more sold, this time to Peramira LLC, a private equity firm. Perhaps, after 45-plus years in fashion, it was time for the partners to scale it back, if not call it quits altogether? Time would tell.

ETERNAL CITY FESTIVITIES

To celebrate those 45 years in fashion, designing clothes that dressed the most elegant women in the world, a Valentino extravaganza took place, the likes of which had not been seen in Europe since the days when kings and queens truly reigned. Merrymaking commenced on the evening of Thursday, July 5, 2007, with a dinner for Valentino's employees at the exclusive Ristorante Gusto, and ended four days later, on Sunday, with a brunch at the French Academy of Villa Medici. It would be three full days of unprecedented indulgence, reportedly costing the fashion house $14 million.

The festivities officially opened on July 6, with the inauguration of a Valentino retrospective, "Valentino in Rome, 45 Years of Style." Valentino had gone through his exhaustive archives, as well as his clients' closets, to pare down his selection to a "mere" 300 garments.

That evening, a post-exhibit gala dinner took place at the Temple of Venus in the Imperial Forum. In its entire 2,000-year history, the forum, dating back to A.D. 135, had never been opened to any event, public or private. Oscar-winning designer Dante Ferretti (*Gangs of New York, The Aviator, The Age of Innocence*) re-created the monument's long-lost columns in fiberglass, involving a special procedure known as anastilosys. High-wire ballerinas, in Valentino red dresses, floated to haunting arias, with the Coliseum, bathed in mauve and red light, acting as a breathtaking backdrop.

Of course, there was a fashion show, staged at 5 P.M., on July 7. A total of 61 dresses were shown, a record number for a haute couture collection; the typical count being no more than 40. Fellow designers, such as Giorgio Armani, Karl Lagerfeld, Donatella Versace, Diane von Fürstenberg, Tom Ford, Carolina Herrera, Zac Posen, Phillip Treacy, and Manolo Blahnik, among others, led a standing ovation. Valentino was seen to be in tears.

At the post-show dinner, which fed a thousand guests, the list of celebrities ran longer than the extended gown trails in the show itself. Princess Caroline of Monaco was there, as was Anna Wintour, editor of *Vogue*. Movie stars, such as Uma Thurman, Anne Hathaway, Sarah Jessica Parker, Sienna Miller, Jennifer Hudson, and Eva Mendes were all in attendance. Socialites included Daphne Guinness, wearing a black-and-white lace flamenco dress with silver platforms and ostrich-feather eyelashes. Allison Sarofim was decked out in a coral-beaded 1960s Valentino, and Lynn Wyatt wore a red taffeta ruffles dress made for her 25 years earlier and found in her attic.

Valentino poses at an exhibition of his best creations in Rome in 2007.

On Sunday, July 8, in a grand finale, Valentino launched his house's latest perfume, Rock 'n Rose Couture.

Of the forty-fifth celebration, Valentino would later say, as reported by Godfrey Deeny, in *Fashion Wear Daily*, "It was a moment of infinite magic and tremendous joy, and I cannot fully express with words how deeply moved I was by the occasion. I received an outpouring of good wishes from all over the world, which brought me great satisfaction. I was very touched that friends, old and new, traveled from far reaches to be a part of the festivities."

Of a possible retirement, nothing was said—although much was whispered.

A LOVE STORY

Both Valentino Garavani and Giancarlo Giammetti are utter, unapologetic control freaks. So it was surprising when writer Matt Tyrnauer approached the partners in late 2004 with the possibility of doing a full-length, "fly-on-the-wall" documentary about their lives, and the two agreed to participate. It would turn out to be a two-year project, starting in the summer of 2005 and taking it through to the 45-years retrospective in July 2007. "They might have thought that I was going to do a fabulous couture documentary, but that was secondary to me," Tyrnauer told Peter Davis, of the Web site PaperMag.com. "It was really about a love story with fashion as the backdrop."

During the filming, Tyrnauer became part of the Valentino entourage. The writer-turned-filmmaker (it was his first professional movie-making experience), traveled everywhere with Valentino, jetting here and there on a private plane, and cruising on the *T.M. Blue One.* Tyrnauer was able to catch Valentino and Giammetti in the most intimate of conversations, times when they could be seen arguing, fighting, and even tearing up. Such confidential filming did not sit well with either partner, particularly Valentino. "He wanted to quit the movie almost every day," Tyrnauer told David Ninh, a special contributor to *The Dallas Morning News.* "The future of the project was frequently questioned. I'm not someone who is comfortable invading other people's spaces. I don't want to seem pushy and tacky, but when you make a documentary, you have to really invade and be aggressive. Whenever we crossed the line and he would lose it, I would feel guilty. But I'm glad that I stuck it out, because the film shows a very real and creative human being."

When Ninh asked Tyrnauer what he had learned most about Valentino while spending time with him, camera on his shoulder, for over 24 months, the documentarian responded, "I've never seen anyone so pure. He's only interested in aesthetics, beauty. . . . the dress. Valentino never had one moment of self-doubt in his life.... He is like a Picasso of design. He's absolutely self-assured, confident."

There were doubts, however, when Valentino saw the final version of the film, before its scheduled release. "They were very undone by the film, having found themselves in a situation they couldn't control," Tyrnauer explained to Ninh. "It was an un-airbrushed version of a very airbrushed life."

Tyrnauer, however, per his film contract, retained final control, and he succeeded in producing the film he wanted to make—a love story. "No one wants to see a puff piece on this man," Tyrnauer explained to Davis. "No one wants to see the packaged Valentino, which is very much the controlled image he put out for decades. People want to see the human, the person."

The movie is not a fashion film, although there are plenty of beautiful clothes worn by plenty of beautiful models. What would be titled *Valentino: The Last Emperor* is about a relationship, both a working one and a personal one, that goes back half a century. "It is about two people with strong characters, sometimes completely different, creating something extraordinary," Giammetti says in the movie. "It is about his [Valentino's] doubts, his insecurities,

---

ELEMENTS OF STYLE

A woman dressed in black and white is to me like a kind of symbol or a signature. In all my collections I always include a black-and-white item, because it provides a sort of rest in the middle of all the colors. At the same time, this kind of punctuation interrupts and thus strengthens a collection. Black and white is just as much a classic as red or beige. A woman who wears black and white is strong and certain to have a great personality—a woman who knows what she wants. That's the sort of woman I admire.

—*from* Valentino's Magic *by Marie Paule Pellé and Patrick Mauriès*

something few people ever see.... Our relationship is beyond finishing each other's sentences. Each knows physically what the other is thinking. There is a psychic bond."

Valentino: The Last Emperor was released at the Venice Film Festival in the summer of 2008. When the 96-minute film ended, the 1,500 attending guests gave a standing ovation. The couturier, it was reported, stood in the balcony with tears in his eyes.

TIME TO SMELL THE ROSES

On September 4, 2007, Valentino Garavani announced his retirement from the world fashion stage. It would become effective, the couturier said, on January 23, 2008, after he presented two final shows: a prêt-à-porter show on October 3, 2007, and a haute couture show in late January 2008. "I want to say, as the English do," Valentino told the *Evening Standard*, "'I would like to leave the party while it is still full.'"

"My future will be filled with new interests and challenges," Valentino, then approaching his seventy-sixth birthday, told Godfrey Deeny. "Some may be linked to fashion, as I have a strong desire to create and support institutions to promote the study of fashion design, and to preserve the history of the art of fashion. It will be a marvelous continuation of this amazing adventure that I had the privilege to have."

Though Valentino talked of the future, one free from the restraints of putting on eight shows a year, and of designing, like any great talent at the end of a career, the couturier was conflicted. "Since that last show [January 21, 2008] I gave the impression that I am quite well," Valentino told Pamela Golbin. "In fact, though, I try to convince myself of that, for what I will miss the most is coming to work. What always interested me most was to be able to sit down and draw."

For Giammetti, too, the transition out of the business of fashion would not be easy. "We have always worked so hard, day in and day out, always projecting ourselves into the future, so that we

Valentino promotes his documentary *Valentino: The Last Emperor* in Rome in 2009. The film captures the designer's drive and unwavering excellence.

have not been able to enjoy the present," he explained to Golbin. "We don't have many memories, for we were always so hectically dealing with what came next, and we had little time for day-to-day living. We never looked back, always forward, without any nostalgia. And now? Now we are in 'detox'—detox from fashion."

In 2005, Valentino, in an interview with Michael Specter, talked of the possibility of retirement, and in so doing, revealed the tension within about what it would mean not to continue to work but to have the freedom to pursue related passions. "What would I do if I didn't do this?" he asked Specter, rhetorically. "I can't just suddenly do nothing. I am tired, though. Eight collections a year, the launches and appearances, drawings and meetings. I cannot let up for a second. You get up in the morning, you are in Rome.

Then Milan. Then Paris. It's all details and deadlines: there are the dresses and fabrics and shoes and fragrances."

As the interview with Specter wound down, Valentino was said to have lowered his voice and declared, "There is also my life. On Monday and Tuesday, I will simply have to steal two days from my work. I have no choice. They called me from Wideville. What has happened at Wideville is hard to believe."

Specter had no idea at first what Valentino was referring to. "There has been an explosion of roses," the couturier continued. "There are thousands. Hundreds of thousands. You cannot imagine it. . . I must go. It is not convenient. Perhaps it is not right. But this garden must be seen now. There are many things you have to do in life, but you cannot ignore the roses. When they demand to be seen, one simply has no choice but go to them."

Valentino Clemente Ludovico Garavani, a universally acknowledged twentieth-century fashion icon who once, almost apologetically, declared, "I love beauty, it's not my fault," would have time enough now to smell his million roses.

Chronology

1932	MAY 11 Valentino Clemente Ludovico Garavani is born in Voghera (Lombardy), Italy.
1952	Valentino receives his diploma from École de la Chambre de la Couture Parisienne.
1959	The House of Valentino opens in Rome, at Via dei Condotti 11.
1960	JULY Valentino meets Giancarlo Giammetti and begins lifelong collaboration.
1967	FEBRUARY 9 Valentino is awarded the Neiman Marcus Prize in Dallas.

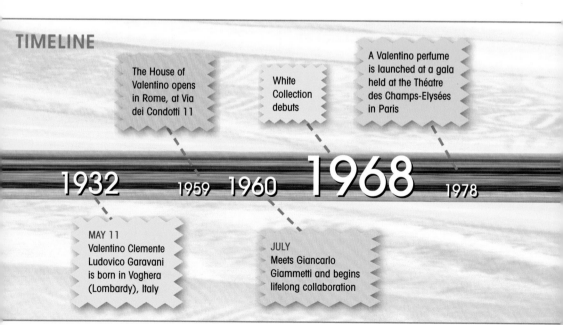

TIMELINE

The House of Valentino opens in Rome, at Via dei Condotti 11

White Collection debuts

A Valentino perfume is launched at a gala held at the Théatre des Champs-Elysées in Paris

1932 1959 1960 **1968** 1978

MAY 11 Valentino Clemente Ludovico Garavani is born in Voghera (Lombardy), Italy

JULY Meets Giancarlo Giammetti and begins lifelong collaboration

1968	Valentino's White Collection debuts.
	OCTOBER 20 Jacqueline Kennedy wears a design from the White Collection for her wedding to Aristotle Onassis.
1975	APRIL 9 Valentino's ready-to-wear line is shown in Paris for the first time, at L'Hôtel George-V.
1978	A Valentino perfume is launched at a gala held at the Théatre des Champs-Elysées in Paris.
1982	Valentino presents his fall-winter collection at the Metropolitan Museum of Art in New York.
1985	Valentino receives Italy's highest honor, the Cavaliere di Gran Croce.
1989	JANUARY 26 Valentino's haute couture collection is presented in Paris for the first time, at École Nationale Supérieure des Beaux-arts.

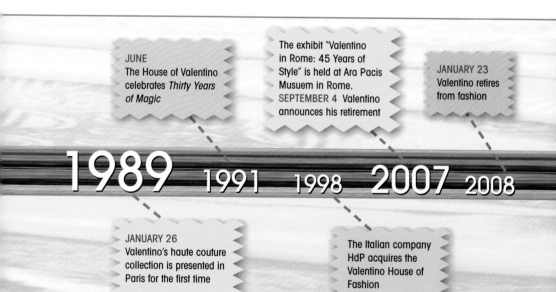

JUNE
The House of Valentino celebrates *Thirty Years of Magic*

The exhibit "Valentino in Rome: 45 Years of Style" is held at Ara Pacis Musuem in Rome.
SEPTEMBER 4 Valentino announces his retirement

JANUARY 23
Valentino retires from fashion

1989 *1991* *1998* **2007** *2008*

JANUARY 26
Valentino's haute couture collection is presented in Paris for the first time

The Italian company HdP acquires the Valentino House of Fashion

1990	Together with Giancarlo Giammetti, Valentino founds L.I.F.E.
1991	JUNE The House of Valentino celebrates *Thirty Years of Magic*.
1993	The Chinese government invites Valentino to present his collection in Beijing.
1996	Valentino is granted the rank of Cavaliere del Lavoro—the equivalent of knighthood.
1998	The Italian company HdP acquires the Valentino House of Fashion.
2002	The Valentino House of Fashion is acquired by Marzotto, a Milan textile manufacturer.
2007	The exhibit "Valentino in Rome: 45 Years of Style" is held at Ara Pacis Musuem in Rome.
	SEPTEMBER 4 Valentino announces his retirement.
2008	JANUARY 23 Valentino retires from fashion.

Glossary

appliqué Ornamental piece of fabric sewn or glued onto another piece of fabric or garment.

atelier Studio or workshop.

bouffant Puffed up or out.

boutique A store showing a selection of merchandise from various designers or an exclusive designer label.

bustle A pad of cork, down, or other type of stuffing worn under a skirt and attached to the back below waist level.

chiffon A light, gossamer-sheer fabric created by tightly twisted yarn.

conglomerate A widely diversified corporation.

corset A close-fitting, boned supporting female undergarment used to achieve a fashionable small waist and to elevate the bust.

couture Individually created, high-fashion clothes.

couturier A male high-fashion clothes designer.

couturiere A female high-fashion clothes designer.

crepe A fabric, natural or synthetic, that has been given a crinkled texture by the use of heat and a crepe weave.

crinoline An open-weave fabric of horsehair or cotton, usually stiffened and used for interlinings and millinery.

fashion plate An illustration of a clothing style, usually appearing in a magazine.

flapper   A young woman of the period following World War I and the following decade who showed freedom from conventions (as in conduct).

franchise   The right to exercise the powers of a corporation.

haute couture   High fashion.

la dolce vita   "The good life," especially identified with Rome in the 1950s and 1960s.

lycra   An artificial fiber with elastic, abrasion-resistant, and stretch-and-recover powers.

muslin   A plain-woven fabric that can be made in a wide range of weights.

oeuvre   A substantial body of work constituting the lifework of an artist.

off-the-rack   Ready-made clothes. Also known as off-the-peg.

organza   A sheer dress fabric.

plait   To braid or interlace.

prêt-à-porter   The French term for "ready-to-wear."

salon   A stylish business establishment or shop.

shirtwaist   The word for a blouse; the female version of a man's shirt.

syndicale   An association of persons officially authorized to undertake a duty or negotiate business (syndicate).

taffeta   A fine, stiff fabric woven from real or artificial silk, with a glossy, iridescent sheen.

toile   A mock-up model of a garment.

zeitgeist   The general intellectual, moral, and cultural climate of an era.

Bibliography

BOOKS

Aragno, Bonizza Giordani. "Chronology," *Valentino's Magic*. New York: Abbeville Press, 1998.

Bailey, Margaret J. *Those Glorious Glamour Years: The Great Hollywood Designs of the 1930s*. Secaucus, N.J.: Citadel Press, 1982.

Batterberry, Michael, and Ariane Batterberry. *Mirror Mirror: A Social History of Fashion*. New York: Holt, Rinehart and Winston, 1977.

Brodkey, Harold. *Avedon: Photographs 1947–1977*. New York: Farrar, Straus & Giroux, 1978.

Carter, Ernestine. *Magic Names of Fashion*. Englewood Cliffs, N.J.: Prentice Hall, 1980.

Cho, Emily, and Linda Grover. *Looking Terrific: Express Yourself through the Language of Clothing*. New York: C.P. Putnam's Sons, 1978.

Ecob, Helen. *The Well-Dressed Woman: A Study in the Practical Applications to Dress of the Laws of Health, Art and Morals*. London: Fowler & Wells, Co., 1893.

Fink, Larry. *Runway*. New York: Powerhouse Books, 2000.

Fraser, Kennedy. *The Fashionable Mind: Reflections on Fashion 1970–1981*. New York: Alfred A. Knopf, 1981.

Frigs, Gini Stephens. *Fashion: From Concept to Consumer*. Englewood Cliffs, N.J.: Prentice-Hall, Inc., 1982.

Golbin, Pamela. *Valentino: Themes and Variations*. New York: Rizzoli, 2008.

Granger, Michele. *Fashion: The Industry and Its Careers*. New York: Fairchild Publications, Inc., 2007.

Green, Nancy L. *Ready-to-Wear and Ready-to-Work: A Century of Industry and Immigrants in Paris and New York*. Durham, N.C., & London: Duke University Press, 1997.

Head, Edith, and Paddy Calistro. *Edith Head's Hollywood.* New York: E. P. Dutton, 1983.

Houck, Catherine. *The Fashion Encyclopedia.* New York: St. Martin's Press, 1982.

Joselit, Jenna Weissman. *A Perfect Fit: Clothes, Character, and the Promise of America.* New York: Henry Holt and Company, 2001.

Ley, Sandra. *Fashion for Everyone: The Story of Ready-to-Wear, 1870s–1970s.* New York: Charles Scribner's Sons, 1975.

McDowell, Colin. *McDowell's Directory of Twentieth Century Fashion.* Englewood Cliffs, N.J.: Prentice Hall, 1985.

Menkes, Suzy, and Matt Tyrnauer. *A Grand Italian Epic: Valentino Garavani.* Cologne & Los Angeles: Taschen GmbH, 2007.

Milbank, Caroline Rennolds. *Couture: The Great Designers.* New York: Stewart, Tabori & Chang, Inc., 1985.

———. *New York Fashion: The Evolution of American Style.* New York: Harry N. Abrams, Inc. 1989.

Morris, Bernadine. *Universe of Fashion: Valentino.* New York: Rizzoli, 1996.

O'Hara, Georgina. *The Encyclopaedia of Fashion.* New York: Harry N. Abrams, Inc., 1986.

Paul, Elizabeth. *Avedon: Photographs 1947–1977.* New York: Farrar, Straus & Giroux, 1978,

Pellé, Marie Paule, and Patrick Mauriès. *Valentino's Magic.* New York: Abbeville Press, 1998.

Reinhold, Elke. "From First Design to Finished Article," *Fashion: The Century of the Designer 1900–1999.* Cologne: Könemann, 2000.

Rethy, Esmerelda De. *Christian Dior: The Glory Years, 1947–1957.* New York: Vendome Press, 2002.

Robinson, Julian. *The Golden Age of Style: Art Deco Fashion Illustration.* New York: Harcourt Brace Jovanovich, 1976.

Rosa, Joseph, ed. *Glamour: Fashion + Industrial Design + Architecture.* San Francisco: San Francisco Museum of Modern Art, 2004.

Seeling, Charlotte. *Fashion: The Century of the Designer 1900–1999.* Cologne: Könemann, 2000.

Tate, Sharon Lee. *Inside Fashion Design.* Upper Saddle River, N.J.: Pearson Prentice Hall, 2004.

Weisberger, Lauren. *The Devil Wears Prada.* New York: Broadway, 2004.

Willett, C., and Phillis Cunnington. *The History of Underclothes.* New York: Dover Publications, Inc., 1992.

NEWSPAPER ARTICLES

Craik, Laura. "Farewell Valentino," *Evening Standard.* January 23, 2008.

Diderich, Joelle. "Fashion Designers Shiver as Economic Crisis Hits," *USA Today.* October 2, 2008.

Horyn, Cathy. "Roman Holiday," *New York Times.* March 30, 2003.

——— . "Q&A: Giancarlo Giammetti," *New York Times.* November 31, 2007.

Magsaysay, Melissa. "Red Carpet Perfection," *Los Angeles Times.* February 28, 2010.

——— . "The Power, Pop of Texture," *Los Angeles Times.* March 8, 2010.

Menkes, Suzy. "Valentino Says Goodbye with Flowers," *New York Times.* January 23, 2008. p 1. [C1]

——— . "YSL Plays Safe While Valentino Shines at Night," *International Herald Tribune.* March 22, 1995.

Morris, Bernadine. "Celebrating 30 Years of Valentino's Couture," *New York Times.* September 24, 1992.

——— . "Youth and Dreams Enliven Paris Style," *New York Times.* March 21, 1990.

Neigher, Julie. "Oscar Visions," *Los Angeles Times.* February 28, 2010.

Ninh, David. "Behind the Scenes on Matt Tynauer's Documentary, 'Valentino: The Last Emperor,'" *The Dallas Morning News.* May 8, 2009.

Phillips, Michael. "'Valentino' No Off-the-Rack Documentary," *Oakland Tribune.* April 1, 2009.

Schiro, Anne-Marie. "Review/Fashion; Valentino in His Element: Glamour Without Camp," *New York Times.* October 18, 1994.

Trebay, Guy. "Paris Diary; Valentino Does What He Wants, and They All Come," *New York Times.* October 10, 2001.

"Valentino Documentary Kept Afloat by Credit Cards," *Reuters.* December 20, 2009.

"Valentino Struggles to Shine Without Its Namesake Designer," *The Wall Street Journal.* October 6, 2009.

MAGAZINE ARTICLES

Aspesi, Natalia. "Valentino, Four Days in Paris," *Il Venerdì di Repubblica.* November 4, 1994.

Bernstein, Jacob. "Age if Exposure," *Women's Wear Daily.* October 13, 2009.

Buck, Joan Juliet. "An Affair Called Valentino," *Vogue.* March 1985.

———— . "Beauty and Soul," Vogue. August 2009.

Collins, Amy Fine. "Don Giammetti," *Vanity Fair.* October 1992. p. 136. [E-44, C5]

Deeny, Godfrey. "Valentino Resigns! *Fashion Wear Daily.* September 4, 2007.

Esterhazy, Louise J. "Louise J. Esterhazy Visits the Chic," *Women's Wear Daily.* January 23, 1981.

Everitt, Lisa. "Valentino Goes After the Less Rich Shopper," *Women's Wear Daily.* May 12, 2008.

Forden, Sara Gay. "Valentino's Big Move," *Women's Wear Daily.* December 1, 1998.

Foxley, David. "Haute Couture's Unlikely Recession Boost," *Vanity Fair.* March 24, 2009.

Goldfarb, Brad. "Valentinohhh!" *Interview.* December 2000.

Guinness, Rebecca. "Gwyneth Paltrow Supports Valentino—Again," *Vanity Fair.* October 28, 2009.

———— . "Valentino Continues to Draw an A-List Crowd," *Vanity Fair.* November 5, 2009.

Koenig, Rhoda. "When Valentino Fêtes His Anniversary, There's No Place Like Rome," *Vogue.* September 1991.

Larocca, Amy. "58 Minutes with Valentino and Giammetti," *New York Magazine.* March 15, 2009.

Lau, Venessa. "Mad About Wu," *W.* March 2010.

Lesser, Guy. "Our Funny Valentino," *Town & Country.* September 1992.

Martin, J.J. "Valentino," *Harper's Bazaar.* June 2006.

Rafferty, Diane. "Valentino," *Connoisseur.* August 1990.

Schiff, Stephen. "Italian Datebook," *The New Yorker.* November 7, 1994.

Shields, Brooke. "Hello, Valentino?" *Interview.* September 1992.

Singer, Sally. "Paris to the Moon," *Vogue.* March 2010.

Specter, Michael. "The Kingdom," *The New Yorker.* September 26, 2005. [C1]

Tyrnauer, Matt. "So Very Valentino," *Vanity Fair.* August 2004.

"Valentino: For the Sophisticated Lady," *Women's Wear Daily.* March 21, 1995.

"Viva Valentino . . . Marking 30 Years in Fashion," *Chicago Tribune.* June 19, 1991.

FILMS

Charlie Rose: A Conversation About the Film "Valentino: The Last Emperor." Charlie Rose, Inc., 2008.

Secret World of Haute Couture. BBC Worldwide Americas, Inc., 2002.

The Devil Wears Prada. Blu-ray, 2006.

The September Issue. Lionsgate. 2009.

Valentino: The Last Emperor. Acolyte Films. 2009.

WEB SITES

"AKC Meet the Breeds: Pug," American Kennel Club. Available online. URL: http://www.akc.org/breeds/pug.index.cfm

Bellis, Mary. "Stitches—The History of Sewing Machines." Available online. URL: http://inventors.about.com/od/sstartinventions/a/sewing_machine.htm

"Capri—Famous Visitors." Available online. URL: http://www.capri.com/en/personaggi

Dargis, Manohla. August 28, 2009. "The Cameras Zoom in on Fashion's Empress." Available online. URL: http://movies.nytimes.com/2009/08/28/movies/28issue.html?partner=Rotten%20Tomatoes&ei=5083

Davis, Peter. "The Chronicles of Truth." Available online. URL: http://www.papermag.com/arts_and_style/2009/03/the-chronicles-of-truth.php

Fortini, Amanda. February 10, 2005. "Defending Vogue's Evil Genius: The Brilliance of Anna Wintour." Available online. URL: http://www.slate.com/id/2113278.

"Garavani Valentino Biography." Available online. URL: http://www.infomat.com/whoswho/garavanivalentino.html

Goldstein, Lauren. "Valentino's Day." Available online. URL: http://www.time.com/time/europe/magazine/2000/0731/valentino.html

Johnson, David. "What Is Haute Couture?" Available online. URL: http://www.infoplease.com/spot/fashionside1.html

Klappholz, Adam. "The Valentino Movie Premiere Draws an A-List Crowd." Available online. URL: http://www.vanityfair.com/online/daily/2009.03.valentino.html

Marcus, Bennett. "Valentino's Pugs Are Mean to Gwyneth Paltrow's Kids, Plan to Blog." Available online. URL: http://nymag.com/daily/fashion/2009/03/valentinos_pugs_dont_like_gwyn.html#ixzz0iDkN3PPe

Nellis, Cynthia. "Day in the Life of a Fashion Professional." Available online. URL: http://fashion.about.com/od/industryinfo/a/dayinthelife.htm

Orecklin, Michelle. February 9, 2004. "The Power List: Women in Fashion, #3 Anna Wintour." Available online. URL: http://www.time.com/time/2004/style/020904/power/3.html.

Pols, Mary. August 28, 2009. "The September Issue: Humanizing the Devil." Available online. URL: http://www.time.com/time/arts/article/0,8599,1918962,00.html

Schrodt, Paul. August 27, 2009. "The September Issue." Available online. URL: http://www.slantmagazine.com/film/film_review.asp?D-4472

Seelye, Katherine. July 19, 1999. "John F. Kennedy Jr., Heir to a Formidable Dynasty." Available online. URL: http://www.nytimes.com/1999/07/19/us/john-f-f-kennedy-jr-heir-to-a-formidable-dynasty.html?

"The Blue Grotto." Available online. URL: http://www.capri.com/en/grotta-azzurra

Tyrnauer, Matt. "The Amazing Odyssey of Directing Valentino: The Last Emperor." Available online. URL: http://www.huffingtonpost.com/matt-tyrnaauer/the-amazing-odyseey-of-di_b_192485.html

Thomas, Pauline Weston. "1950s Fashion Glamour C20th Fashion History 1950s." Available online. URL: http://www.fashion-era.com

"Valentino." Available online. URL: http://www.vanityfair.com/culture/features/2009/04/proust-valentino200904

"Valentino." Available online. URL: http://www.fashionencyclopedia.com/To-Vi/Valentino.html

"Valentino Garavani." Available online. URL: http://www.YourNewFragrance.Com

"Valentino Garavani: A Biography." Available online. URL: http://kunkun.tripod.com/valentino.htm

"Valentino Retires on a Red Dress Catwalk." Available online. URL: http://www.fashionrat.com/valentino-retires-on-ared-dress-catwalk/

"Valentino: The Last Emperor and His Houses." Available online. URL: http://hookedonhouses.net/2010/02/07/valentino-the-last-emperor-and-his-houses/

Weber, Caroline. December 3, 2006. "Fashion-Books: Review of 'IN VOGUE: The Illustrated History of the World's Most Famous Fashion Magazine (Rizzoli).'" Available online. URL: http://www.nytimes.com/2006/12/03/books/Weber2.t.html?

Zakaria, Namrata Sharma. "Valentino, Italy's Top Designer." Available online. URL: http://www.expressindia.com/news/fullstory.php?news id=39139

 # Further Resources

Blackman, Cally. *100 Years of Fashion Illustration.* London: Laurence King Publishers, 2007.

Borrelli, Laird. *Fashion Illustration by Fashion Designers.* San Francisco: Chronicle Books, 2007.

Eceiza, Laura. *Atlas of Fashion Designers.* Beverly, Mass.: Rockport Publishers, 2008.

Garcia, Nina. *The Little Black Book of Style.* New York: HarperCollins, 2007.

Teen Vogue. *The Teen Vogue Handbook.* New York: Penguin Young Readers Group, 2009.

Travers-Spencer, Simon, and Zarida Zaman. *The Fashion Designer's Directory of Shape and Style.* Hauppauge, N.Y.: Barron's Educational Series, 2008.

Zoe, Rachel, and Rose Apodaca. *Style A to Zoe.* New York: Grand Central Publishing, 2007.

WEB SITES

Fashion-Era
http://www.fashion-era.com
Contains over 700 illustrated pages of fashion, costume, clothing, and social history. Loaded with everything fashion.

Fashion Games
http://www.fashiongames247.com
Fashion games for people who love fashion. Mix and match paper outfits.

Top 50 Blogs in Fashion
http://www.networkedblogs.com/topic/fashion.
Identifies 50 blog sites dealing with the complete range of fashion trends and issues.

Top 10 Teen Clothing Web Sites

http://www.lovetoknow.com/top10/teen-clothing.html

Listing of top sites, such as Teen Clothes at Love To Know, Teen clothes at eHow, teenvogue, PACSUN.com, etc.

Picture Credits

Index

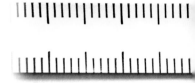

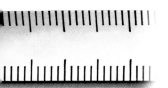 # About the Author

RONALD A. REIS has written young-adult biographies of Eugenie Clark, Jonas Salk, Lou Gehrig, Mickey Mantle, Ted Williams, Sitting Bull, Buffalo Bill Cody, and Simón Bolívar, as well as books on the Dust Bowl, the Empire State Building, the New York subway system, African Americans and the Civil War, the World Trade Organization, and the Great Depression and the New Deal, all for Chelsea House. He is the technology department chair at Los Angeles Valley College.